Aunt Phil's Trunk Volume Two

Student Workbook

Bringing Alaska's history alive!

By
Laurel Downing Bill

Special credit and much appreciation to Nicole Cruz for her diligent efforts to create the best student workbook and teacher guide available for Alaska history studies.

Aunt Phil's Trunk LLC, Anchorage, Alaska
www.auntphilstrunk.com

International Standard Book Number 978-1-940479-33-0
Printed and bound in the United States of America.

First Printing 2017
First Printing Second Edition 2017
First Printing Third Edition 2018

Photo credits on the front cover, from top left: Native shaman with totem, Alaska State Library, Case and Draper Collection, ASL-P-39-782; Eskimo boy, Alaska State Library, Skinner Foundation, ASL-P44-11-002; Prospector, Alaska State Library, Skinner Foundation, ASL-P44-03-15; Athabascan woman, Anchorage Museum of History and Art, Crary–Henderson Collection, AMHA-b62-1-571; Gold miners, Alaska State Library, Harry T.Becker Collection, ASL-P67-052; Chilkoot Pass, Alaska State Library, Eric A. Hegg Collection, ASL-P124-04; Seal hunter, Alaska State Library, George A. Parks Collection, ASL-P240-210; Women mending boat, Alaska State Library, Rev. Samuel Spriggs Collection, ASL-P320-60; Students in class, Alaska State Library, Wickersham State Historical Site, ASL-P277-015-029.

TABLE OF CONTENTS

Table of Contents

Welcome to *Aunt Phil's Trunk Volume Two* Workbook for Students!

Read the chapters associated with each Unit. Then complete the lessons for that Unit to get a better understanding of Alaska's people and the events that helped shape Alaska's future.

I hope you enjoy your journey into Alaska's past from the years 1900 to 1912.

Laurel Downing Bill, author

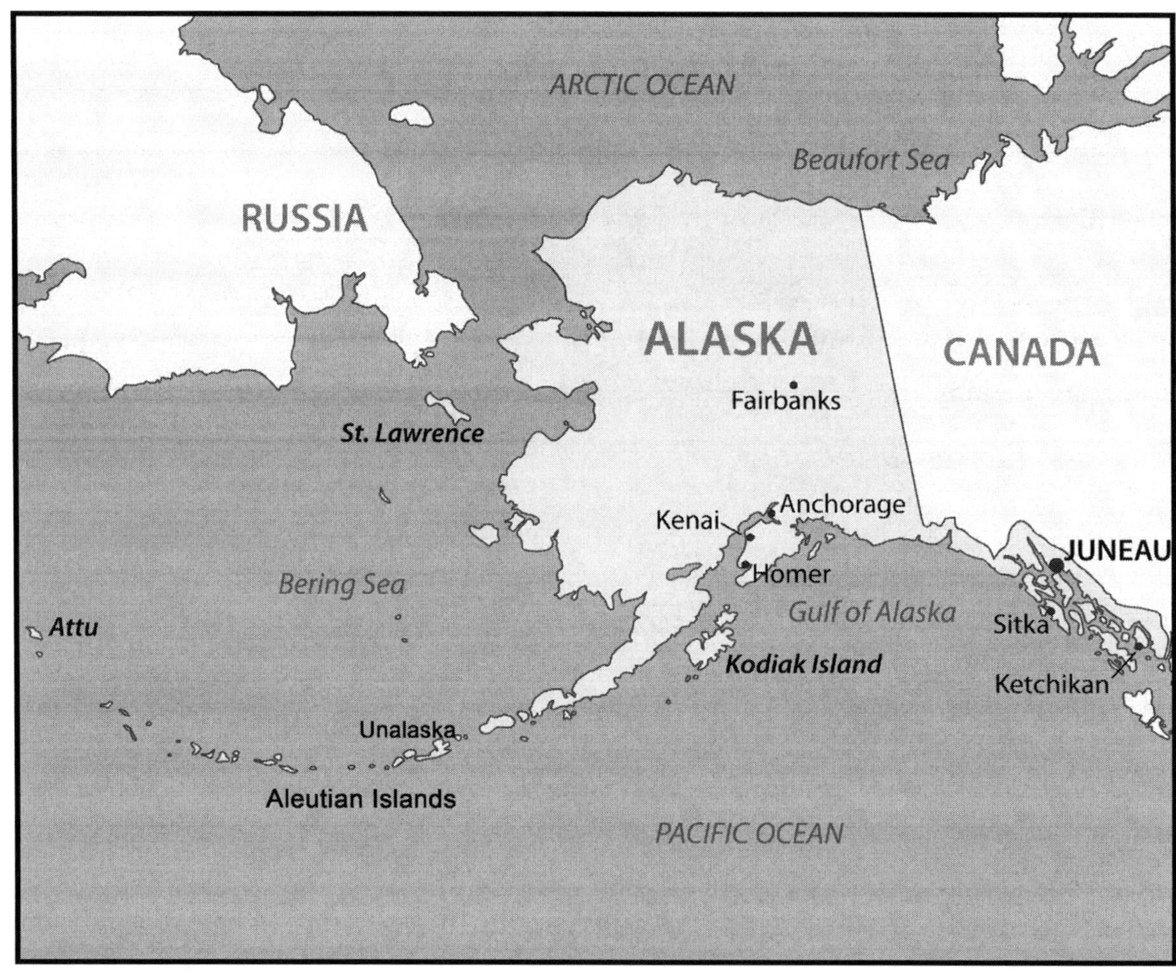

Instructions for using the Aunt Phil's Trunk Alaska History Curriculum

The *Aunt Phil's Trunk* Alaska History Curriculum is designed to be used in grades 4-8. High school students can use this curriculum, also, by taking advantage of the essay and enrichment activities throughout the book. The next few pages give further instruction on how to use this curriculum with middle school students, high school students and in classroom settings.

This curriculum can be taught in multiple grade levels by having your older students complete all reading, study guide work and enrichment activities independently. Students of all grade levels can participate in daily oral review by playing games like Jeopardy or Around the World.

This curriculum was developed so that students not only learn about Alaska's past, but they will have fun in the process. After every few lessons, they can test their knowledge through word scramble, word search and crossword puzzles.

Notes for parents with younger students:

Enrichment Activities occasionally direct your child to watch educational videos on YouTube.com or link to other Websites to learn more about the topic that they are reading about in the lesson. You may want to supervise younger children while they are using the Internet to be sure that they do not click on any inappropriate content. This also provides a good opportunity to discuss Internet safety with your child/children.

How to use this workbook at home

Aunt Phil's Trunk Alaska History Curriculum is designed to be used in grades 4-8. High school students can use this curriculum, also, by taking advantage of the essay and enrichment activities throughout the book. The next page gives further instruction on how to use this curriculum with high school students.

This curriculum can be taught in multiple grade levels by having your older students complete all reading, study guide work and enrichment activities independently. Students of all grade levels can participate in daily oral review by playing games like Jeopardy or Around the World.

For Middle School Students:

1. **Facts to Know:** Read this section in the study guide with your student(s) before reading the chapter to get familiar with new terms that they will encounter in the reading.

2. **Read the chapter:** Read one chapter aloud to your student(s) or have them read it aloud to you. Older students may want to read independently.

3. **Comprehension Questions:** Younger students may answer the comprehension questions orally or write down their answers in the study guide. Use these questions to test your student(s) comprehension of the chapter. Older students should answer all questions in written form.

4. **Discussion Questions:** Have your student(s) answer these questions in a few sentences orally. Come up with follow-up questions to test your student(s) understanding of the material. Older students may answer discussion questions in written essay form.

5. **Map Work:** Some chapters will contain a map activity for your student(s) to learn more about the geography of the region that they are learning about.

6. **Enrichment and Online References:** (Optional) Assign enrichment activities as you see fit. Many of the online references are from the Alaska Humanities Forum website (http://www.akhistorycourse.org). We highly recommend this website for additional information, project ideas, etc.

7. **Unit Review:** At the end of a unit, your student will complete Unit Review questions and word puzzles in the study guide. Students should review all the chapters in the unit before completing the review. Parents may want to assist younger students with the word puzzles.

8. **Unit Test:** (Optional) There is an optional test that you can administer to your student(s) after they have completed all the unit work.

How to use this workbook for high school

1. **Facts to Know:** Your student(s) should read this section in the study guide before reading the chapter to get familiar with new terms that they will encounter.

2. **Read the chapter:** Your student(s) can read aloud or independently.

3. **Comprehension Questions:** Use these questions to test your student(s) comprehension of the chapter. Have your high schoolers write out their answers in complete sentences.

4. **Discussion Questions:** Have your student(s) answer these questions in a few sentences orally or write out their answer in essay form.

5. **Map Work:** Some chapters will contain a map activity for your student(s) to learn more about the geography of the region that they are learning about.

6. **Enrichment and Online References:** Once your high schooler has completed all the reading and study guide material for the chapter, assign additional reading from the enrichment material using the online links or book lists. Encourage your student(s) to explore topics of interest to them.

Many of the online references are from the Alaska Humanities Forum website. We highly recommend this website for additional information, project ideas, etc.

7. **Unit Review:** At the end of a unit, your student will complete Unit Review questions and word puzzles in their study guide. Students should review all the chapters in the unit before completing the review.

8. **Unit Test:** (Optional) There is an optional test that you can administer to your student(s) after they have completed all the unit work.

9. **Oral Presentation:** (Optional) Assign a 5-minute oral presentation on any topic in the reading. Encourage your student(s) to utilize the additional books and online resources to supplement the information in the textbook. Set aside a classroom day for your student(s) to share their presentations.

10. **Historical Inquiry Project:** Your student(s) will choose a topic from the reading to learn more about and explore that topic through library visits, museum trips, visiting historical sites, etc.

Visit https://www.nhd.org/how-enter-contest for detailed information on how to put together a historical inquiry project. You may even want to have your students enter the national contest.

How to use this workbook in the classroom

Aunt Phil's Trunk Alaska History Curriculum was created for homeschooling families, but it also can work well in a co-op or classroom setting. Here are some suggestions on how to use this curriculum in a classroom setting. Use what works best for your classroom.

1. **Facts to Know:** The teacher introduces students to the Facts to Know to familiarize the students with terms that they will encounter in the chapter.

2. **Read the chapter:** The teacher can read the chapter aloud while the students follow along in the book. Students also may take turns reading aloud.

3. **Comprehension Questions:** The teacher uses these questions to test the students' comprehension of the chapter. Students should write out the answers in their study guide and the teacher can review the answers with the students in class.

4. **Discussion Questions:** The teacher chooses a few students to answer these questions orally during class. Alternatively, teachers can assign these questions to be completed in essay form individually and answers can be shared during class.

5. **Map Work:** Some chapters will contain a map activity for your students to learn more about the geography of the region that they are learning about. Have your students complete the activity independently.

6. **Enrichment and Online References:** Assign enrichment activities as you see fit.

7. **Daily Review:** Students should review the material for the current unit daily. You can do this by asking review questions orally. Playing review games like Jeopardy or Around the World is a fun way to get your students excited about the material.

8. **Unit Review:** At the end of a unit, your student will complete Unit Review questions and word puzzles in the study guide. Have students review all the unit chapters before completing.

9. **Unit Test:** (Optional) There is an optional test that you can administer to your students after they have completed all the unit work.

10. **Oral Presentation:** (Optional) Assign a 5-minute oral presentation on any topic in the reading. Encourage your students to utilize the additional books and online resources to supplement the information in the textbook. Set aside a classroom day for students to share their presentations.

11. **Historical Inquiry Project:** Your student(s) will choose a topic from the reading to learn more about and explore that topic through library visits, museum trips, visiting historical sites, etc.

Visit https://www.nhd.org/how-enter-contest for detailed information on how to put together a historical inquiry project. You may even want to have your students enter the national contest.

How to grade the assignments

Our rubric grids are designed to make it easy for you to grade your students' essays, oral presentations and enrichment activities. Encourage your students to look at the rubric grid before completing an assignment as a reminder of what an exemplary assignment should include.

You can mark grades for review questions, essay tests and extra credit assignments on the last page of each unit in the student workbook. Use these pages as a tool to help your students track their progress and improve their assignment grades.

Unit Review Questions

Students are given one point for each correct review and fill-in-the-blank question. Mark these points on the last page of each unit in the student workbook.

Essay Test Questions

Students will complete two or more essay questions at the end of each unit. These questions are designed to test your students' knowledge about the key topics of each unit. You can give a student up to 20 points for each essay.

Students are graded on a scale of 1-5 in four categories:

1) Understanding the topic
2) Answering all questions completely and accurately
3) Neatness and organization
4) Grammar, spelling and punctuation

Use the essay rubric grid on page 11 as a guide to give up to 5 points in each category for every essay. Mark these points for each essay on the last page of each Unit Review in the student workbook.

Word Puzzles

Word puzzles that appear at the end of the Unit Reviews count for 5 points, or you can give partial points if the student does not fill in the puzzle completely. Mark these points under the extra category on the last page of each Unit Review in the student workbook.

Enrichment Activities

Most lessons contain an enrichment activity for further research and interaction with the information in the lesson. You can make these optional or assign every activity as part of the lesson. You can use the provided rubric on page 12 to give up to 5 points for each assignment. Mark these points under the extra category on the last page of each Unit Review in the student workbook.

Oral Presentations

You have the option of assigning oral presentations on any topic from the unit as extra credit. If you choose to assign oral presentations, you can use the provided rubric to grade your student on content and presentation skills. Discuss what presentation skills you will be grading your student on before each presentation day.

Some examples of presentation skills you can grade on include:

- Eye contact with the audience
- Proper speaking volume
- Using correct posture
- Speaking clearly

Use the oral presentation rubric grid on page 12 as a guide to give up to 10 points. Mark these points under the extra category on the last page of each Unit Review in the student workbook.

Rubric for Essay Questions

	Beginning 1	Needs Improvement 2	Acceptable 3	Accomplished 4	Exemplary 5
Demonstrates Understanding of the topic	Student's work shows incomplete understanding of the topic	Student's work shows slight understanding of the topic	Student's work shows a basic understanding of the topic	Student's work shows complete understanding of the topic	Student's work demonstrates strong insight about the topic
Answered questions completely and accurately	Student's work did not address all of the questions	Student answered all of the questions with some accuracy	Student answered all questions with close to 100% accuracy	Student answered all questions with 100% accuracy	Student goes beyond the questions to demonstrate knowledge of the topic
Essay is neat and well organized	Student's work is sloppy and unorganized	Student's work is somewhat neat and organized	Student's essay is neat and somewhat organized	Student's work is well organized and neat	Student demonstrates extra care in organizing the essay and making it neat
Essay contains good grammar and spelling	Student's work is poorly written and hard to understand	Student's work contains some grammar, spelling and punctuation mistakes, but not enough to impede understanding	Student's work contains only 1 or 2 grammar, spelling or punctuation errors	Student's work contains no grammar, spelling or punctuation errors	Student's work is extremely well-written

Rubric for Oral Presentations

	Beginning 1	Needs Improvement 2	Acceptable 3	Accomplished 4	Exemplary 5
Preparation	Student did not prepare for the presentation	Student was somewhat prepared for the presentation	Student was prepared for the presentation and addressed the topic	Student was well-prepared for the presentation and addressed important points about the topic	Student prepared an excellent presentation that exhibited creativity and originality
Presentation Skills	Student demonstrated poor presentation skills (no eye contact, low volume, appears disinterested in the topic)	Student made some effort to demonstrate presentation skills (eye contact, spoke clearly, engaged audience, etc.)	Student demonstrated acceptable presentation skills (eye contact, spoke clearly, engaged audience, etc.)	Student demonstrated good presentation skills (eye contact, spoke clearly, engaged audience, etc.)	Student demonstrated strong presentation skills (eye contact, spoke clearly, engaged audience, etc.)

Rubric for Enrichment Activities

	Beginning 1	Needs Improvement 2	Acceptable 3	Accomplished 4	Exemplary 5
	Student's work is incomplete or inaccurate	Student's work is complete and somewhat inaccurate	Student completed the assignment with accuracy	Student's work is accurate, complete, neat and well-organized	Student demonstrates exceptional creativity or originality

UNIT 1: GLIMMERS OF GOLD

LESSON 1: BORDER HEATS UP

FACTS TO KNOW

Border – The geographical dividing line between two political or geographical entities
Survey – To examine and record an area's physical geography so one can create a border, map or plan
Thomas Riggs – Crew chief for the International Boundary Commission and governor of Alaska from 1918-1921
International Boundary Commission – The group in charge of keeping a visible border between two countries

COMPREHENSION QUESTIONS

1) Why was it a major problem that no border officially existed between Alaska and Canada in 1867? ______________________________

____
____
____

2) How did the Klondike Gold Rush cause an even greater need for a more defined border between Alaska and Canada around 1897? ______________________________

____
____
____
____

3) Why did the stampeders disagree with the Canadians on the exact border? __________

____
____
____
____

4) How did the United States and Canada finally settle the border dispute in 1904? ______

____
____
____
____

5) How was the border marked? How long did it take to create the visible border? ______

____

____

____

____

DISCUSSION QUESTION

(Discuss this question with your teacher or write your answer in essay form below. Use additional paper if necessary.)

Describe the disagreement between Michael J. Heney and Stikine Bill Robinson.

____

____

____

____

____

____

____

____

____

____

____

____

____

____

____

LEARN MORE

Look for this book in your local library:
Blazing Alaska's Trails. Brooks, Alfred H., Fairbanks: University of Alaska Press, 1953.

Map Activity

Using Page 16 of your textbook, trace the Alaska-Canada border onto the map below. Mark the following towns: 1) Prince Rupert 2) Skagway 3) Juneau 4) Atlin

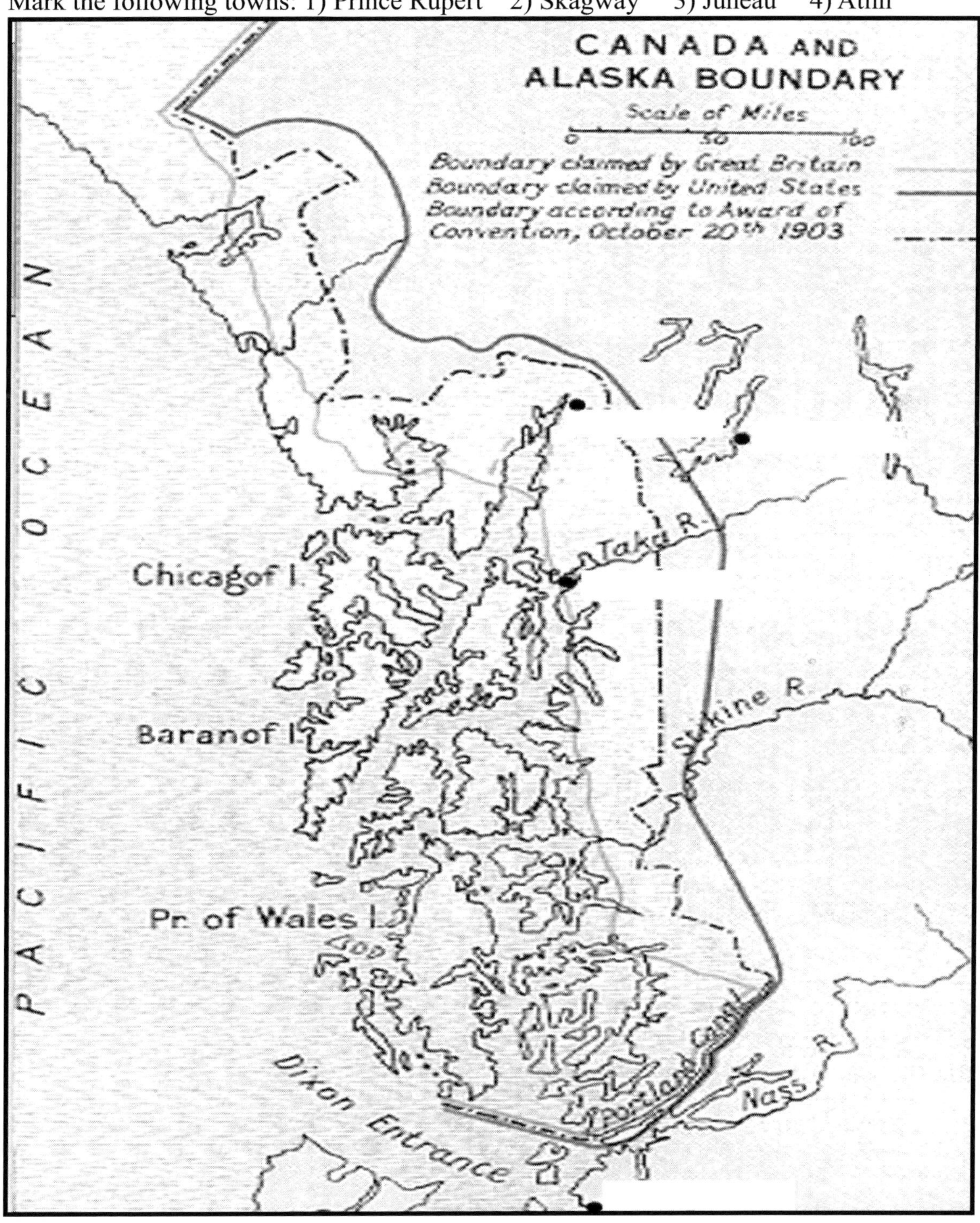

UNIT 1: GLIMMERS OF GOLD

LESSON 2: GOLD RUSH ENTERTAINERS ARRIVE

FACTS TO KNOW

Opera House – Dawson City's first theater
Vaudeville – Type of entertainment that is a mixture of comedy, song and dance
Monte Carlo – First theater in Dawson City to be powered by electricity
Palace Grand – One of Dawson City's largest theaters built by Arizona Charlie Meadows

COMPREHENSION QUESTIONS

1) Name two famous entertainers who performed in Nome. For what were they famous?

____

____

____

2) How did Dawson City become the largest city in Canada in 1898? ______________

____

____

____

3) Describe Dawson's first opera house. What did it look like? What kind of performances did it showcase? ______________________________

____

____

____

4) What happened to the Opera House in 1897? ______________________

____

____

____

5) Name three popular shows performed at the Palace Grand.

____

____

____

DISCUSSION QUESTION

(Discuss this question with your teacher or write your answer in essay form below. Use additional paper if necessary.)

Why do you think entertainment was such a big industry in places like Nome and Dawson City during the gold rushes?

ENRICHMENT ACTIVITY

Listen to samples of Klondike Gold Rush music by visiting http://alaska-klondikemusic.com/

LEARN MORE

Look for this article at your local library:
"The Homes of Nome," in *The Alaska Journal* 4 (1) (Winter 1974): 17-20. Murtagh, William J.

UNIT 1: GLIMMERS OF GOLD

LESSON 3: GOLDEN HEART CITY GROWS

FACTS TO KNOW

Elbridge Truman Barnette – Called E.T., Barnette is credited with establishing Fairbanks in Alaska's interior

James Wickersham – District judge in Alaska who saw value in Fairbanks and moved his offices there in 1903

Felix Pedro – Italian prospector who discovered gold in the Tanana Valley

COMPREHENSION QUESTIONS

1) What led E.T. Barnette to start a trading post along the Chena River? What happened when he first set out to bring supplies to Alaska's interior? ______________________

____

____

____

____

2) How did Barnette eventually start his trading post? Why did he name the spot Fairbanks?

____

____

____

____

3) How long did it take Felix Pedro to find gold in the Tanana Valley? How many claims had he staked by 1903? ______________________

____

____

____

4) How did E.T. Barnette promote the Fairbanks gold rush? How did the stampede later become a problem for him? ______________________

____

____

____

____

5) When Judge Wickersham decided to move his judicial headquarters from Eagle to Fairbanks, how did that affect the population of the Interior town? What was his impression of Fairbanks as recorded in his diary in 1903?

____
____
____
____

6) As the city of Fairbanks grew, what important transportation system materialized?

____
____

DISCUSSION QUESTION

(Discuss this question with your teacher or write your answer in essay form below. Use additional paper if necessary.)

What did Elbridge Barnette do after he sold two-thirds of his interest in the trading post to Northern Commercial Company? Why did this sale benefit Fairbanks?

____
____
____
____
____
____
____
____
____
____
____
____
____
____
____

ENRICHMENT ACTIVITY

Imagine that you, like Elbridge Barnette, are establishing a new trading post in a high traffic area of Alaska during the gold rush. Write a journal entry about your exciting adventures. What is the area like? Who did you meet? What challenges did you face?

LEARN MORE

Look for these books at your local library:
E.T. Barnette: The Strange Story of the Man Who Founded Fairbanks, Terrance Cole. Anchorage: Alaska Northwest Publishing Company, 1981.

Frontier Politics: Alaska's James Wickersham. Atwood, Evangeline. Portland, Oregon: Binford & Mort, 1979.

TIME TO REVIEW

Review Chapters 1-3 of your book before moving on to the Unit Review. See how many questions you can answer without looking at your book.

Courtesy Alaska State Library

This April 1903 view of E.T. Barnette's trading post, known as Barnette's Cache, shows that Barnette and his crew had built a warehouse, far left, cabin and had started building a store. A few months later, Barnette received word that Felix Pedro had found large quantities of gold. The town of Fairbanks soon would rise around this trading post.

UNIT 1: GLIMMERS OF GOLD

REVIEW LESSONS 1-3

Write down what you remember about:

Border ____

____

Survey ____

____

Thomas Riggs ____

____

International Boundary Commission ____

____

Opera House ____

____

Vaudeville ____

____

Monte Carlo ____

____

Palace Grand ____

____

Elbridge Truman (E.T.) Barnette ____

____

James Wickersham ____

____

Felix Pedro ____

____

Fill in the blanks.

1) Alaska's border with ________________ is one of the great feats of wilderness ____________. Marked by __________________ and a __________________ 20 feet wide, the boundary is _____________ miles long.

2) ________________ officials wanted ownership of ___________and ___________, which would allow ________________ access to the ____________ gold fields without crossing ________________ soil. But ________________ flooding into Skagway didn't agree. _______________ thought that the head of Lake Bennett, another 12 miles north, should be the boundary between the two territories.

3) A _________________________ was established to finally resolve the boundary issue in __________. The ___________________ claimed a continuous stretch of coastline, unbroken by the deep fiords of the region. ___________________ demanded control of the heads of certain fiords, especially the __________ Canal, as it gave access to the ____________ River.

4) A formal treaty was signed in 1908 between the ___________________ and ________________________setting up the ________________________________ to mark the boundary officially.

5) When Circle City and Fortymile were emptied as a result of the _______________, ____________ City became the center of entertainment. After the historic discovery of gold on _____________ Creek in August _________, ___________ City grew up from a marshy swamp near the confluence of the _______________ and _____________ rivers.

6) Dawson's first theater was grandiosely called the _______________. It was in reality a ____________ building with a bar and gambling rooms in front and a theater in the rear. One of Dawson's finest theaters, The ______________________, was built by Arizona Charlie Meadows.

7) What kind of entertainment was offered to the patrons? Some examples include:

____

____.

8) ___________________, located on the ____________ River in Interior Alaska, didn't begin as a well-thought-out plan for civilization. It began as a wilderness _____________ set up in the wrong place at the wrong time of year.

9) ____________________________ thought a trading post sitting at a strategic spot with heavy traffic just might make him a rich man, and a trading operation at ____________ would be accessible by river in the summer and by ________________ year-round.

10) After hearing about the trading post along the __________ River, ______________ _________________, the newly appointed U.S. district judge for the territory, suggested ___________________ rename his post in honor of a man the judge mightily admired: Republican Sen. Charles W. ______________ of Indiana.

Courtesy Alaska State Library

This photo of men surveying the Canada-Alaska border between 1907-1913 shows surveyors marking the line between the two countries somewhere around Mount St. Elias.

Notice the headgear the man sitting on the ground is wearing. Mosquitoes and biting gnats were a constant problem in the wilderness.

Glimmers of Gold

Crossword Puzzle

Read Across and Down clues and fill in blank boxes that match numbers on the clues

Across

3 E.T. Barnette sent him to Dawson to spread the word of the Fairbanks gold strike
8 The first theater in Dawson
11 To examine and record an area's physical geography so one can create a border/map
12 Barnette's riverboat that sank in St. Michael in the summer of 1901
14 The Golden Heart City
16 Judge who moved his judicial headquarters from Eagle to Nome
17 What E.T. Barnette first called his new settlement in Alaska's Interior
19 When ice melts and leaves rivers in the spring
22 A settlement that explodes with population in a short time due to something like a gold rush
25 These creatures swarmed Barnette and his group as they chopped down trees to clear space for his trading post
26 Name of Barnette's trading post
27 The country that rules Canada
30 City that grew up on a swampy marsh after gold was discovered on Bonanza Creek
31 A varied mixture of people or things like songs
34 The valley where the Fairbanks gold strike occurred
35 This was the mode of transportation between some of the mines near Fairbanks
36 This gold rush brought stampeders into the area that became Dawson
37 Crew chief for the International Boundary Commission
38 The geographical dividing line between two political or geographical entities
39 Some people thought this animal, named Wise Mike, was the most talented actor in Dawson
40 Owner of the Chinese Theatre in Hollywood

Down

1 Man who envisioned a settlement on the belief merchants in gold camps prospered more than miners
2 One of the biggest dangers to a gold-rush town
4 First theater in Dawson to be lit by electricity
5 A group of entertainers who travel and perform together
6 Country that borders Alaska
7 He played piano in the Northern Saloon in Nome when he was 8 years old
9 This theater was built by Arizona Charlie Meadows
10 Place where E.T. Barnette originally wanted to build a trading post
11 The con man that organized criminal activities along the railroad route from Southeast Alaska into Canada along the White Pass Trail
13 River along which the town of Fairbanks grew
15 Name of shallow-draft boat that E .T. Barnette had made in St. Michael
18 Places where gold is dug out of the ground
20 Depart quickly, hurry away
21 The man who found gold in sufficient quantity in 1902 that it drew people into Alaska's interior

Glimmers of Gold

Crossword Puzzle

Down (Continued)

23 Number of streets staked out through the woods in Fairbanks when Wickersham arrived in April 1903
24 Variety show of comedy, singing and dancing offered in Dawson City
25 A drawing of an area of land showing physical features, cities, roads, etc.
27 Type of gun Canadians mounted on the summits of Chilkoot and White passes during border dispute
28 Felix Pedro's mining companion
29 Captain that dropped E .T. Barnette and his supplies off along the Chena River
32 The canal in southeast Alaska that both the Americans and Canadians wanted control over
33 One of Broadway's leading beauties

UNIT 1: GLIMMERS OF GOLD

UNIT TEST

Choose *two* of the following questions to answer in paragraph form. Use as much detail as possible to completely answer the question. Use extra paper in back of the book if needed.

1) Why was it so important to establish an exact Alaska-Canada border? What was the dispute between Canada and the United States? How was the dispute resolved?

2) What was gold-rush entertainment like in places like Nome, Circle City and Dawson? What kind of performers were popular? Describe two famous places of entertainment you read about in Chapter 2.

3) Describe Elbridge Barnette's journey to establish the city of Fairbanks. Why did he set out to the Interior? What obstacles did he face? Why did he name the trading post Fairbanks?

Aunt Phil's Trunk Volume Two

UNIT 1: GLIMMERS OF GOLD

Review Questions ______ (possible 11 pts.)
Fill-the-Blanks ______ (possible 10 pts.)

Unit Test

Essay 1

Demonstrates understanding of the topic ______ (possible 5 pts.)
Answered the questions completely and accurately ______ (possible 5 pts.)
Composition is neat ______ (possible 5 pts.)
Grammar and Spelling ______ (possible 5 pts.)

Essay 2

Demonstrates understanding of the topic ______ (possible 5 pts.)
Answered the questions completely and accurately ______ (possible 5 pts.)
Composition is neat ______ (possible 5 pts.)
Grammar and Spelling ______ (possible 5 pts.)

Subtotal Points ______ (possible 61 pts.)

Extra Credit

Word Puzzle ______ (5 pt. per completed puzzle)
Complete an Enrichment Activity ______ (possible 5 pts.)
Oral presentation ______ (possible 10 pts.)

Total Extra Credit ______

Total Unit Points ______

GRADE CHART

A 55-61+ points

B 49-54 points

C 43-48 points

D 37-42 points

UNIT 2: CROOKS RUN RAMPANT

LESSON 4: BLUE PARKA BANDIT STRIKES AGAIN
LESSON 5: TURN-OF-THE-CENTURY JUSTICE

Note: Read both chapters 4 and 5 before completing this lesson.

FACTS TO KNOW

Blue Parka Bandit – A notorious robber who preyed on the miners in Fairbanks
Hendrickson – Identity of the Blue Parka Bandit
Thornton – A horse thief that was a prisoner on the *Lavelle Young* with Hendrickson
Miners' Code – The law of the land in gold rush camps

COMPREHENSION QUESTIONS

1) Who was the last person robbed by the Blue Parka Bandit? What happened when the Blue Parka Bandit tried to rob him? ______________________________

____

____

____

2) How did law enforcement figure out the identity of the Blue Parka Bandit? ________

____

____

____

____

____

3) What precautions did the guards aboard the *Lavelle Young* take to prevent the prisoners from escaping? How did they escape? ______________________________

____

____

____

____

4) How did Hendrickson and Thornton get caught? ______________________________

____

____

____

____

5) Explain how the miners' code worked. How were disputes handled? How were guilty parties punished? ______________________________

____

____

____

6) How were people married in gold rush camps when there were no judges or ministers?

____

____

____

DISCUSSION QUESTION

(Discuss this question with your teacher or write your answer in essay form below. Use additional paper if necessary.)

What do you think your hometown would be like if it were run by the miners' code? Do you think there would be more or less crime? Explain your answer.

____

____

____

____

____

____

____

____

____

____

____

ENRICHMENT ACTIVITY

Imagine that you are a miner in Nome during the gold rush era, and your camp put you in charge of writing the miners' code for your camp. How would you settle disputes? Who decides if someone is innocent or guilty? What punishments will you put into place? Is there an appeals process?

LEARN MORE

Look for this book at your local library:
The Alaskan Gold Fields. By Dunham, Sam C., Anchorage: Alaska Northwest Publishing Company, 1984. Book insert in THE ALASKA JOURNAL 14 (1) (Winter 1984).

UNIT 2: CROOKS RUN RAMPANT

LESSON 6: TOMBSTONE TEMPORARILY TRANSPLANTED

FACTS TO KNOW

Ed Schieffelin – A prospector from Arizona who searched for a highway of gold
Wyatt Earp – Infamous participant in the shootout at OK Corral
Tombstone – Historic city in Arizona where the OK Corral is located
Dexter Saloon – Wyatt Earp's "Second Class Saloon" in Nome

COMPREHENSION QUESTIONS

1) Where did Ed Schieffelin find silver before coming to Alaska? How long did he search?

____

____

____

____

____

2) What was his theory about finding gold in the Yukon? Was his prospecting trip successful? What happened? _______________________

____

____

____

____

____

3) What happened in the shootout at the OK Corral? _______________

____

____

____

____

4) What brought Wyatt Earp to Nome? What did he do there? __________

____

____

____

____

____

5) Why did Wyatt Earp go back to California during the winter? When did he leave Alaska for good? ____

____

____

____

DISCUSSION QUESTION

(Discuss this question with your teacher or write your answer in essay form below. Use additional paper if necessary.)

Stories like Wyatt Earp have been made into exciting movies. If you were a movie maker, what part of history would you like to turn into a movie? Why?

____

____

____

____

____

____

____

____

____

____

____

____

____

____

ENRICHMENT ACTIVITY

Read more about Wyatt Earp by visiting https://www.britannica.com/biography/Wyatt-Earp or http://www.pbs.org/wgbh/americanexperience/features/timeline/wyatt/
Write a paragraph about what you learned.

LEARN MORE

Learn more about Nome by visiting: http://www.akhistorycourse.org/americas-territory/travel-travelers-agree-that-nomes-golden-lining-is-in-its-history

TIME TO REVIEW

Review Chapters 4-6 of your book before moving on to the Unit Review. See how many questions you can answer without looking at your book.

UNIT 2: CROOKS RUN RAMPANT

REVIEW LESSONS 4-6

Write down what you remember about:

Blue Parka Bandit ____

____

Hendrickson ____

____

Thornton ____

____

Miners' Code ____

____

Ed Schieffelin ____

____

Wyatt Earp ____

____

Tombstone ____

____

Dexter Saloon ____

____

Fill in the blanks:

1) The ______________________________ had struck again. Alaskans felt they had a good joke on ______________________, a popular Episcopalian missionary who was in the last party robbed by the daring highwayman.

2) When the citizens of Fairbanks saw the ____________________ and ____________________ board the __________________ under the watchful eye of a federal marshal, they breathed a collective sigh of relief that the two wouldn't be in their town jail another winter.

3) The dinner gong sounded at 5:30 p.m. on October 6 while the ___________________ and ______________________ were tied up at the ___________ City wood yard to take on fuel. A guard burst through the door and announced that The ____________________ had escaped.

4) __________________________ engineered the escape. Somehow, he'd obtained a ____before leaving ________________. He divided a brass tube into two pieces and used one as a key to unscrew the bolts locking the 30-pound ______________ on their feet.

5) A practical application of frontier democracy called the _________________ was the only law that ruled the Far North. Each ____________ decided matters of common concern by _________________.

6) After all the ____________________ was weighed, the _______________ would render a verdict: Murder was punished by ________________; stealing meant a sound ______________ or _________________. The guilty had no notice of _______________, no bill of exceptions and no ______________________.

7) After searching for more than a decade, _______________________________ finally discovered silver in the state of __________________. Following his discovery, he founded the _____________ Mining District, which evolved into __________________________.

8) When the silver dwindled, _______________________ was determined to repeat his success with ___________ in Alaska. He had an interesting theory that somewhere in Alaska a ___________________________ crossed the Yukon – a continuation of a great mineral belt that girdled the world from Cape Horn to Asia.

9) _____________________ fled Arizona to go to ___________ because he was under suspicion for murder following the notorious 1881 massacre of _________________ at the __________________ and later the shooting of Frank Stillwell.

10) There were conflicting reports of what happened during the famous shootout at ______________________. The surviving ______________________ charged that the ____________ brothers and _________________ stalked their victims, some of whom were unarmed, and shot first without provocation. But the __________ and _____________ claimed that the ___________________ were waiting for them and cocked their pistols first.

11) According to a letter found in the basement of the Juneau federal jail, ____________ wanted to settle down in ____________________. But a posse met his ship and told him ____________________________________.

12) After _________________________ arrived in Nome, he built the ______________ saloon and billed it as ____ _________.

13) After _________________________ and his partner, ____________, left Nome for good, they lived in California where he spent years writing ________________________ and ____.

Law enforcement often rested in the Miners' Code when prospectors discovered gold in the Klondike region, Nome and Fairbanks. But as this photograph taken in Sitka shows, a jail – along with the Baranof Castle, Marine barracks and custom house – was built by the Russians after they settled in Southeast Alaska in the early 1800s. The Russians brought their brand of justice with them when they colonized parts of Alaska, and the U.S. War Department carried out laws following the Alaska purchase in 1867.

Early Law and Order

Word Search

Find the words listed below

A S N E E H A M N U P T I A L S T O R L

P K N N B E R N I L V C Q F J E X C L Y

O N M O P Z E P Q N N G D T I A U J F N

H A K T M Q B J P Z E N R K R T R G K I

S B C S R J B T O N W R D O R J S P Q L

I R E B I P O C I P O Y S P T E N K C E

B I X M H K R F Z F L Z A C B I X O D F

P A L O O R E G O N B O O T O O B Q M F

V F C T T L H H F U W R Z G T D F T N E

N Z I N R B P U I K D U L R L E E O E I

O L Y I E P Y W A C G F R T Y V A H R H

S J S B S N A M Y A W H G I H P L R G C

K P I H S M A E T S E H C I B M W A P S

C F L U F H S O D E F G Q Q Q S V J C R

I W V B T X E L G N U O Y E L L E V A L

R E E J R J O U T E F F D R L G V L C P

D M R B P G R N B Z Q W Q V C P Y D A D

N N S I F U L H E S R O T C E P S O R P

E J K Q T Y K G X M Y T O Y K V M G H W

H J O G Q S N O T N A L C H I P V A E F

HENDRICKSON
FAIRBANKS
OREGON BOOT
NUPTIALS
SCHIEFFELIN
SILVER

HIGHWAYMAN
BISHOP
LAVELLE YOUNG
TOMBSTONE
STEAMSHIP
GOLD

ROBBER
PROSPECTORS
MINERS CODE
WYATT EARP
CLANTONS
NOME

UNIT 2: CROOKS RUN RAMPANT

UNIT TEST

Choose *two* of the following questions to answer in paragraph form. Use as much detail as possible to completely answer the question. Use extra paper in back of the book if needed.

1) Describe what happened on the *Lavelle Young* on October 6, 1905.

2) How did the miners' code work? Who made decisions? How were guilty parties punished?

3) Who was Ed Schieffelin? Where was he from? What was his theory about gold in Alaska? Did he prove his theory to be true?

4) What happened at the O.K. Corral in Tombstone? Who was involved? What were the conflicting accounts?

UNIT 2: CROOKS RUN RAMPANT

Review Questions ______ (possible 8 pts.)
Fill-the-Blanks ______ (possible 13 pts.)

Unit Test

Essay 1
- Demonstrates understanding of the topic ______ (possible 5 pts.)
- Answered the questions completely and accurately ______ (possible 5 pts.)
- Composition is neat ______ (possible 5 pts.)
- Grammar and Spelling ______ (possible 5 pts.)

Essay 2
- Demonstrates understanding of the topic ______ (possible 5 pts.)
- Answered the questions completely and accurately ______ (possible 5 pts.)
- Composition is neat ______ (possible 5 pts.)
- Grammar and Spelling ______ (possible 5 pts.)

Subtotal Points ______ (possible 61 pts.)

Extra Credit
- Word Puzzle ______ (5 pt. per completed puzzle)
- Complete an Enrichment Activity ______ (possible 5 pts.)
- Oral presentation ______ (possible 10 pts.)

Total Extra Credit ______

Total Unit Points ______

GRADE CHART

A 55-61+ points

B 49-54 points

C 43-48 points

D 37-42 points

UNIT 3: LAW AND ORDER

LESSON 7: ALASKA'S FIRST LAWMEN

FACTS TO KNOW

Frank Canton – First lawman in Alaska's interior
Lawman – A person in charge of enforcing the law
Capt. Michael Healy – First U.S. Revenue Marine cutter commander to make regular patrols into harsh arctic waters
Revenue Cutter – A sea vessel used to enforce federal law under the U.S. Revenue Marine branch

COMPREHENSION QUESTIONS

1) How did Frank Canton become the first lawman in Alaska's interior? ______________

____

____

____

____

2) What happened on his way to Circle City? ______________________________

____

____

____

____

3) Why was it difficult for him to do his job when he got to Circle City? ____________

____

____

____

____

4) Why was Frank Canton discharged as deputy? What was revealed after his death?

____

____

____

____

____

5) How did Michael Healy enforce the law? ______________________________

____

____

____

6) In what other ways did Healy serve the people of Alaska? ________________

____

____

____

DISCUSSION QUESTION

(Discuss this question with your teacher or write your answer in essay form below. Use additional paper if necessary.)

What challenges did Alaska's early lawmen face?

____

____

____

____

____

____

____

____

____

____

____

ENRICHMENT ACTIVITY

Although Michael Healy was honored for all the good that he did, we read about two accounts of him treating people badly aboard his ship. History is full of people that we remember for the great things they did, but they did some bad things, too. Can you think of one example? If not, do some research at the library or online. Write a paragraph or two about both the good and bad things that this person did in his/her life. Conclude your writing with what that person is most remembered for doing.

LEARN MORE

Read more about Capt. Michael Healy and the U.S. Revenue cutter *Bear* by visiting http://www.akhistorycourse.org/northwest-and-arctic/1871-1897-arctic-explorations

UNIT 3: LAW AND ORDER

LESSON 8: JUDGE'S LIGHT SHINES ON

FACTS TO KNOW

Judge James Wickersham – One of the most influential figures in Alaska history
Traveling court – A group of jurors and other lawmen that traveled to decide a case where there were not enough people to summon sufficient jurors
Alfred Noyes – The corrupt judge in Nome who left mining disputes unsettled to take money for himself
Denali – Native Alaskan word for Mt. McKinley (Judge Wickersham was the first to organize a trip to climb Denali)

COMPREHENSION QUESTIONS

1) What new system did Judge James Wickersham begin in 1900? Why did he see a need for this? ____

____

____

____

2) It was said, jokingly, in the Northwest that __________________ was sent to Alaska to get him out of ____________________ politics. If so, ____________________ tossed a whole hornet's nest into Alaska, for he was the storm center of more ________________________ and is credited with having ________________________ ________________________________ than any other of Alaska's early public figures.

3) Describe the mess that Judge Wickersham was hired to clean up in Nome.

____

____

____

____

4) According to his journal entries, how did Judge Wickersham resolve the mess in Nome?

____

____

____

____

____

5) Name at least two of the "firsts" attributed to Judge Wickersham. ________________

____

____

____

6) While serving Alaska, Wickersham found the Library of Congress had no Alaska section. What did he do about this? ____

____

____

____

DISCUSSION QUESTION

(Discuss this question with your teacher or write your answer in essay form below. Use additional paper if necessary.)

Why is Judge James Wickersham an important figure in Alaska's history?

____

____

____

____

____

____

____

____

____

____

____

____

ENRICHMENT ACTIVITY

Put together your own mini bibliography of Alaska history. Visit your local library or use your home computer to search for at least 5-10 books, Websites or magazine articles on Alaska history. Write down the title, author, date of publication, place of publication and publication company for each resource.

LEARN MORE

Look for this book at your local library:
Frontier Politics: Alaska's James Wickersham. By Evangeline Atwood. Portland, Oregon: Binford & Mort, 1979.

Early Alaska Lawmen

Crossword Puzzle

Read Across and Down clues and fill in blank boxes that match numbers on the clues

Across

3 To appease the anger or anxiety of someone
5 First U.S. Revenue cutter to regularly ply Alaska's waters in an effort to bring law and order
9 Keeping someone from harm
11 Wickersham moved to this new center of gold mining in 1903
15 First U. S. Revenue cutter commander to make regular patrols into harsh arctic waters
16 Town where Judge Wickersham held the first traveling court
21 She interpreted for the captain of the U.S. Revenue cutter *Bear*
22 The people of Fairbanks honored Judge Wickersham with this when their courthouse was dedicated on July 4, 1904
26 Name of crooked judge in Nome
27 An upright bar, post or frame forming a support or barrier used on U. S. Revenue cutters for disciplinary measures
29 To say that something may not be true
30 A formal charge or accusation of a serious crime
34 Another name for Mt. McKinley
35 Something that causes much discussion, disagreement or argument
38 The real name of the first lawman in Interior Alaska
39 Interior Alaska's first lawman was appointed as this (official title)
40 Where Interior Alaska's first lawman spent his first winter in 1898
41 Judge Wickersham produced one newspaper using this machine
42 Wickersham amassed 10,380 items of Alaska literature for this to be included in the Library of Congress
43 A light, fast coastal patrol boat
44 Not satisfied with something

Down

1 To haul up and lash securely
2 To confine someone as a punishment for a crime
4 Judge Wickersham's first official judicial headquarters was in this town
7 Small cord
8 Number of successive terms that Alaskans elected Judge Wickersham as their delegate to Congress
10 One who illegally occupies property to which another has a legal claim
12 Town in Southeast Alaska where prisoners from the Interior were taken for trial
13 U.S. Revenue cutters often served as these
14 Unrestrained by law
17 The people along the Siberian coast that raised reindeer
18 Planks, bars or logs where something heavy may be slid or rolled along
19 Relating to the government or public affairs of a country
20 An illegal or dishonest scheme for obtaining money

Early Alaska Lawmen

Crossword Puzzle

Down (Continued)

23 Those who work as sailors
24 Type of animals brought from Siberia to Alaska to help feed Natives and miners
25 Wickersham lived in this Alaska town until his death in 1939
28 A person who seeks to promote human welfare
31 Where Interior Alaska's first lawman was to set up his headquarters and build a jail
32 District judge of newly organized Third Judicial Division of Alaska
33 To clear someone of blame
36 First lawman in Interior Alaska
37 An application to a higher court for a decision to be reversed

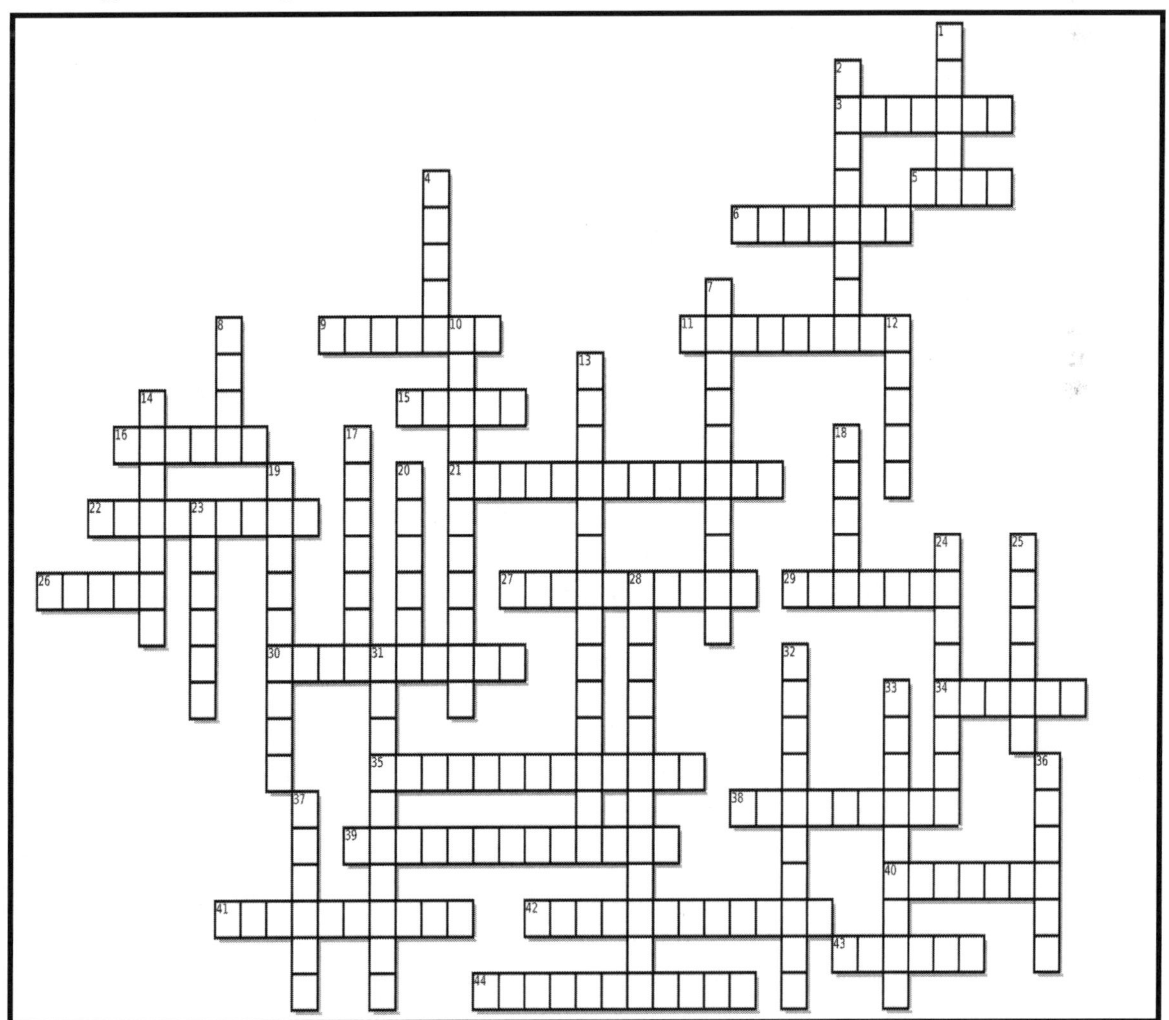

UNIT 3: LAW AND ORDER

LESSON 9: *CITY OF SEATTLE* TURNS TO PIRACY
LESSON 10: INMATE NO. 594

Note: Read both chapters 9 and 10 before completing this lesson.

FACTS TO KNOW

Totem poles – Tall Native American sculptures mostly carved on logs that often tell a story or represent an event

City of Seattle – A steamship that carried a group from Seattle to Sitka to steal a totem pole

Robert Stroud – A miner who killed a man in Juneau and wrote books about birds and bird diseases while serving a life sentence

Alcatraz – Famous maximum-security prison on Alcatraz Island in the San Francisco Bay

COMPREHENSION QUESTIONS:

1) Why did the group from Seattle travel to Sitka to find a totem pole? What happened when they got there? ____

____

____

____

____

2) Who did they steal the totem pole from? What did this group demand from the thieves? What did they receive in return? ______________________________

____

____

____

____

3) Where was the totem pole kept after it was stolen? What happened to it in 1938?

____

____

____

____

____

4) Why was Robert Stroud sent to prison for seven years? ____________________

____

____

____

5) What did Robert Stroud do right before his release that caused him to be sentenced to death? How did his death sentence get changed to a life sentence in solitary confinement? ____

____

____

____

6) What did Robert Stroud do while he served his sentence in Leavenworth? What was his nickname while imprisoned at Alcatraz? ____________________________

____

____

DISCUSSION QUESTION:

(Discuss this question with your teacher or write your answer in essay form below. Use additional paper if necessary.)

Do you think that the Tlingit people were properly compensated for the stolen totem pole? Explain your answer.

____

____

____

____

____

____

____

____

____

____

____

____

____

____

____

ENRICHMENT ACTIVITY

The totem pole that was stolen from the Raven Clan was craved in honor of a special woman called Chief-to-all-Women in 1790. Draw or paint your own totem pole either on a sheet of paper or on an empty paper towel roll. Present your totem pole or drawing to your class, and explain what it represents.

Read the link from the Learn More section for inspiration.

LEARN MORE:

Read more about how totem poles are made by visiting https://www.warpaths2peacepipes.com/native-indian-art/how-to-make-a-totem-pole.htm

Courtesy Alaska State Library

Southeast Alaska communities are home to many totem poles. Unfortunately many of the totems in Kake, such as those in this photo taken in the late 1890s, were destroyed when missionaries misunderstood their meanings and thought them idols created by the Native people.

UNIT 3: LAW AND ORDER

LESSON 11: ALASKA'S FIRST SERIAL KILLER

FACTS TO KNOW

Edward Krause – Alaska's first serial killer
Treadwell Gold Mining Company – At one time one of the largest gold mining companies in the world
Sequestered jury – When a judge orders that a jury be isolated from the public for the duration of a trial

COMPREHENSION QUESTIONS

1) Who first suspected that Edward Krause had something to do with the disappearance of James Christie? Why did they suspect Krause? ______________________________

____

____

____

____

2) How did the police discover that Krause was responsible for more than one disappearance? ______________________________

____

____

____

____

3) What was uncovered about Edward Krause during the yearlong investigation?

____

____

____

____

4) Who were Edward Krause's supporters? What did they believe about Krause? Why were they dangerous? ______________________________

____

____

____

____

5) What two firsts in Alaska court history occurred during the Edward Krause trials?

6) What was the verdict in the Krause case? What happened after sentencing?

DISCUSSION QUESTION

(Discuss this question with your teacher or write your answer in essay form below. Use additional paper if necessary.)

"The true story of Krause's criminal enterprises and their extent will never be known. But if the story could ever be told, it would undoubtedly be one of the most startling in the annals of American crime history," stated a letter to the Department of Justice, written by attorney James Smiser of Juneau.

What did attorney Smiser mean by this statement? Why will the whole story never be told?

TIME TO REVIEW

Review Chapters 7-11 of your book before moving on to the Unit Review. See how many questions you can answer without looking at your book.

MAP ACTIVITY

Find the following places from Krause's story on the map below. Use the lesson for help, then write the name of each Southeast Alaska town in its proper box on the map.

1) Juneau
2) Petersburg
3) Ketchikan
4) Wrangell

Also locate 5) Sitka, the town from which a totem pole was stolen from the Raven Clan in the late 1890s.

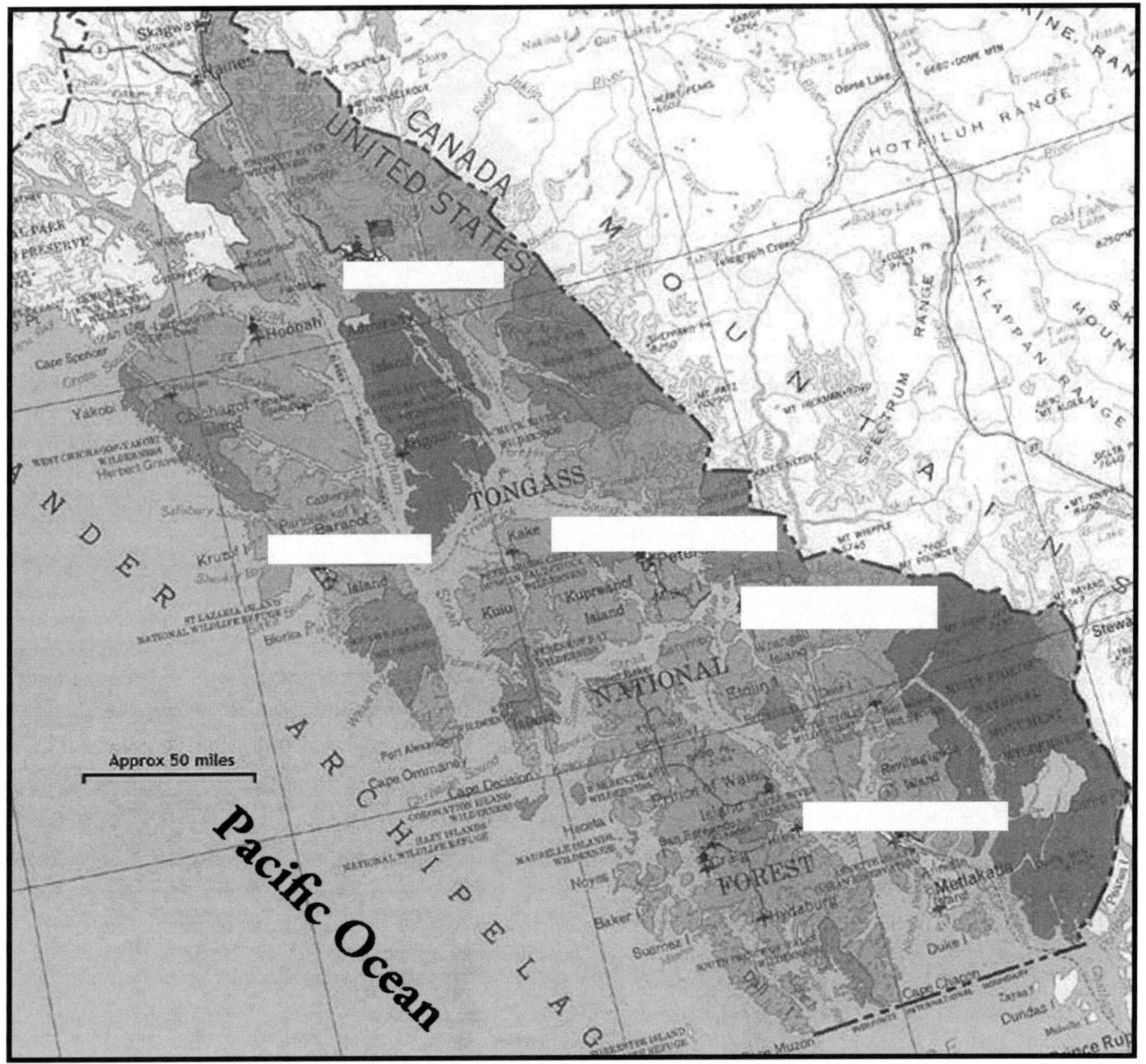

UNIT 3: LAW AND ORDER

REVIEW LESSONS 7-11

Write down what you remember about:

Frank Canton ____

____

Lawman ____

____

Capt. Michael Healy ____

____

Revenue Cutter ____

____

Judge James Wickersham ____

____

Traveling court ____

____

Alfred Noyes ____

____

Denali ____

____

Totem pole ____

____

City of Seattle ____

____

Robert Stroud ____

____

Alcatraz ____

____

Edward Krause ____

____

Treadwell Gold Mining Company ____

____

Sequestered jury ____

____

Fill in the blanks:

1) ____________________ found his work cut out for him when he headed to ____________________ to serve as the first lawman in Interior Alaska in the late 1890s.

2) By the time he reached his new post, ______________ found that most of the miners had moved on to ________________. Their exodus meant that city coffers were limited, so the lawman had no _______________ with which to operate. He also found that no one in the community wanted to board federal prisoners for $3 a day, nor act as jailers.

3) Life wasn't easy for Alaska's early lawmen. U.S. marshals didn't have ____________ to pursue, capture or hold evildoers who committed crimes in the territory. Due to the logistics of covering __________________________________, suspects sometimes roamed at large for months, perhaps years, before being taken into custody. There was also the problem of transporting the prisoners to ______________ for trial.

4) ____________________________ set up Alaska's first official _______________ court in the laundry building in _______________ in 1900.

5) ________________________ was called upon to travel to ______________ to clear up disputed ________________. When ____________________, an influential Republican, arranged to have President William McKinley appoint __________________ as judge of one of three newly created judicial districts in Alaska, the stage was set to separate hardworking miners from their claims.

6) The steamer, ___________________, carried a delegation on board in 1899 that stole a _________________ from the ____________________ in the city of ______________, Alaska.

7) After murdering a man in __________________ in 1909, ____________________ was sentenced to ____________ years in prison. Just before his scheduled release, he _________________________________ and was sentenced ______________________. His mother spoke to ___________________________, who convinced her husband ____________________________ to change his sentence to solitary confinement for life.

8) His nickname, "___________________________," came from his life on the rock. And his monumental work, "___________________________," published in 1942, still is regarded as an authoritative source.

9) ___________________ showed up at the ___________________ Mining Company and asked for a mine worker named ___________________, and that's the last time anyone ever saw the unfortunate miner.

10) To protect the jury from intimidation by Krause's still-active _______________, the judge ___________________ the jury during the trial – a first in Alaska court history. Krause's trial also marked the first extensive use in Alaska of _______________ ___________________________ experts.

Law enforcement in Alaska was not a glamorous way of life, as this 1903 photo of the Ofice of the Deputy U.S. Marshal in Candle City shows.

Law and Order Southeast Alaska Style

Word Scramble Puzzle

Please unscramble the words below

	Scrambled word	Answer	Clue
1.	tmteo		Item that people on board the City of Seattle stole from Southeast Alaska in 1899.
2.	nvera		Clan of people in Sitka that demanded payment for their stolen property.
3.	rnoeeip		Famous Seattle square where a Tlingit monument was placed in 1899.
4.	tuosdr		Last name of convict who wrote a research book on canaries
5.	acrlatza		Famous prison on a rocky island near San Francisco.
6.	woinls		U.S. president who commuted Birdman's sentence from death to life imprisonment.
7.	auerks		Alaska's first serial killer.
8.	letlwreda		Famous gold mine in Juneau.
9.	koptnneri		Well-known detective agency hired to investigate the disappearance of a man named Christie.
10.	mehotarsede		Person who claimed the reward for the apprehension of Krause on Admiralty Island.

UNIT 3: LAW AND ORDER

UNIT TEST

Choose *three* of the following questions to answer in paragraph form. Use as much detail as possible to completely answer the question. Use extra paper in back of the book if needed.

1) Name three challenges that early lawmen faced in Alaska.

2) What were three important things that Judge James Wickersham did while serving Alaska? Explain the significance of each one.

3) Why would some people call the *City of Seattle* a pirate ship? Describe what happened in 1899 when the steamship traveled to Sitka.

4) Who was the Birdman of Alcatraz? How did he earn this nickname? How did he end up in Alcatraz?

5) What was Edward Krause convicted of in 1917? How did he get caught? What two firsts in Alaska court history occurred during his trial?

UNIT 3: LAW AND ORDER

Review Questions	______	(possible 15 pts.)
Fill-the-Blanks	______	(possible 10 pts.)

Unit Test

Essay 1

Demonstrates understanding of the topic	______	(possible 5 pts.)
Answered the questions completely and accurately	______	(possible 5 pts.)
Composition is neat	______	(possible 5 pts.)
Grammar and Spelling	______	(possible 5 pts.)

Essay 2

Demonstrates understanding of the topic	______	(possible 5 pts.)
Answered the questions completely and accurately	______	(possible 5 pts.)
Composition is neat	______	(possible 5 pts.)
Grammar and Spelling	______	(possible 5 pts.)

Essay 3

Demonstrates understanding of the topic	______	(possible 5 pts.)
Answered the questions completely and accurately	______	(possible 5 pts.)
Composition is neat	______	(possible 5 pts.)
Grammar and Spelling	______	(possible 5 pts.)

Subtotal Points ______ (possible 85 pts.)

Extra Credit

Word Puzzle	______	(5 pt. per completed puzzle)
Complete an Enrichment Activity	______	(possible 5 pts.)
Oral presentation	______	(possible 10 pts.)

Total Extra Credit ______

Total Unit Points ______

GRADE CHART

A 76-85+ points

B 68-75 points

C 59-67 points

D 50-58 points

UNIT 4: ROUTES TO RESOURCES

LESSON 12: ARIZONA EDITOR MAKES MARK ON ALASKA

FACTS TO KNOW

John Clum – Editor of the *Tombstone Epitaph* and the first appointed post office inspector for Alaska

Post Office Inspector – The person who regulates and oversees the post offices

COMPREHENSION QUESTIONS

1) Name three of John Clum's ventures. ______________________________

____

____

2) Describe John Clum's duties as the post office inspector. Was this an easy job? Explain your answer. ______________________________

____

____

____

3) Use your book to fill in the blanks and follow John Clum's route to establish post offices throughout Alaska:

He established post offices in Southeast Alaska at _________ Camp, the last station before the Chilkoot Pass, ______________ and ____________. Clum reestablished the post office at Haines and reorganized the offices at _____________ and ____________.

Then he started down the Yukon River.

Clum and his son traveled to ___________________. From ________________, he traveled to ______________ via _________________. At __________________, he established the first new post office of the Interior, and then traveled 18 miles down the ________________ River to set up another post office at _____________, located at the mouth of Seventymile River.

His next stop was _________________ City, where the first post office on the Yukon River had been established in 1896. He found the post office there, under Jack McQuesten, "in good order." On July 1, 1898, he and his son boarded the steamer ___________ for its maiden voyage down the Yukon to ________________, stopping to establish post offices at ______________________________

______________________________.

DISCUSSION QUESTION

(Discuss this question with your teacher or write your answer in essay form below. Use additional paper if necessary.)

Why do you think mail service was so important to Alaskans during this time?

MAP ACTIVITY

There are three maps on the next two pages that show where John Clum traveled to set up new post offices in Alaska. The map on Page 54 shows the route he took in Southeast Alaska. The top map on Page 55 shows the route along the Yukon River and the bottom map shows Prince William Sound, Cook Inlet and the Aleutian Islands. See if you can mark on the maps the names of the towns where Clum established post offices.

LEARN MORE

Learn more about the start of the post office in Alaska by visiting http://www.akhistory-course.org/americas-territory/alaskas-heritage/chapter-4-13-communications

Mark the following settlements where John Clum founded new post offices along the Chilkoot Trail in Southeast Alaska: 1) Dyea 2) Canyon 3) Sheep Creek

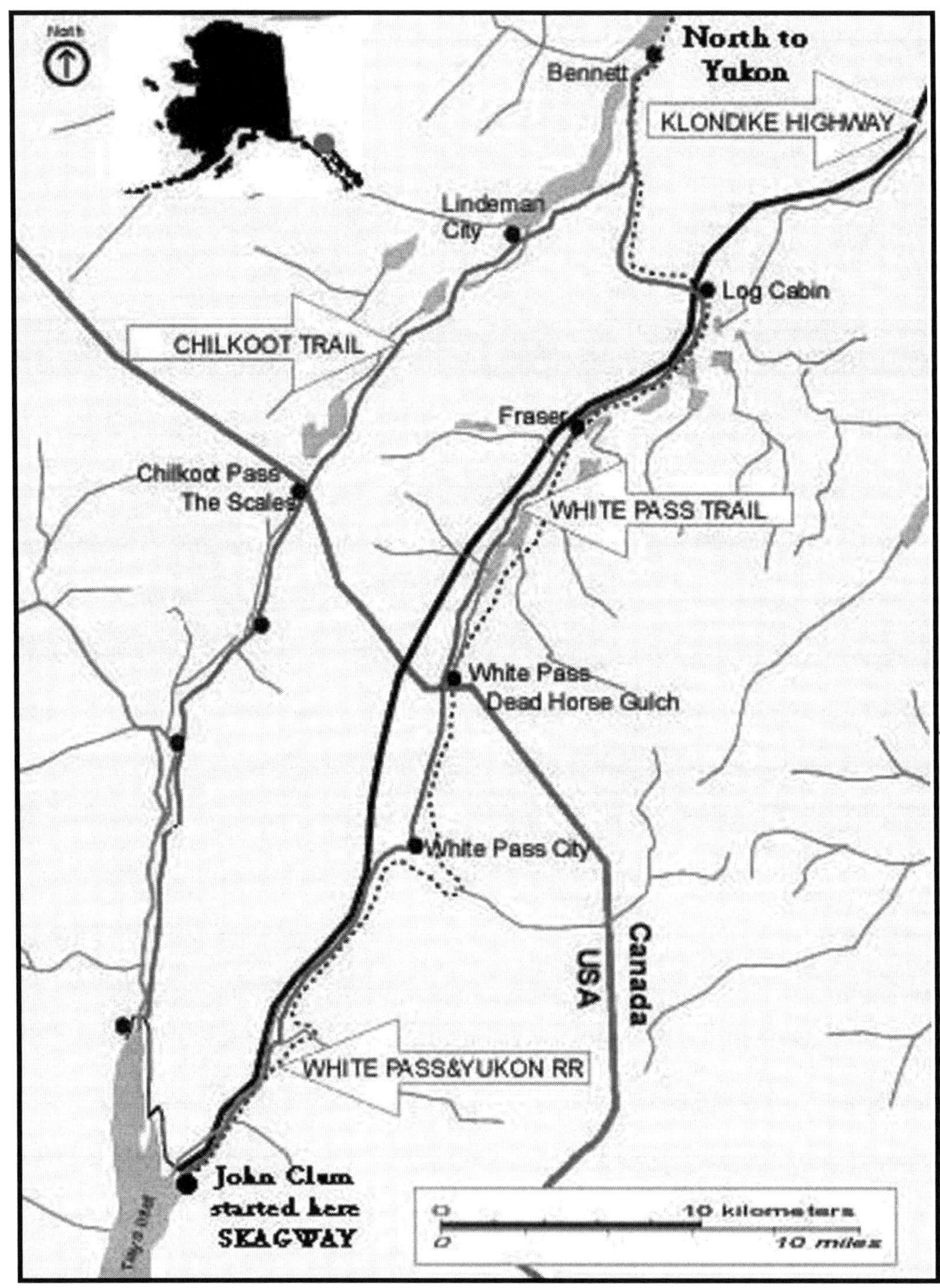

Mark the following settlements where John Clum founded new post offices along the Yukon River: 1) Eagle 2) Fort Yukon 3) Rampart 4) Koyukuk 5) Nulato 6) Anvik

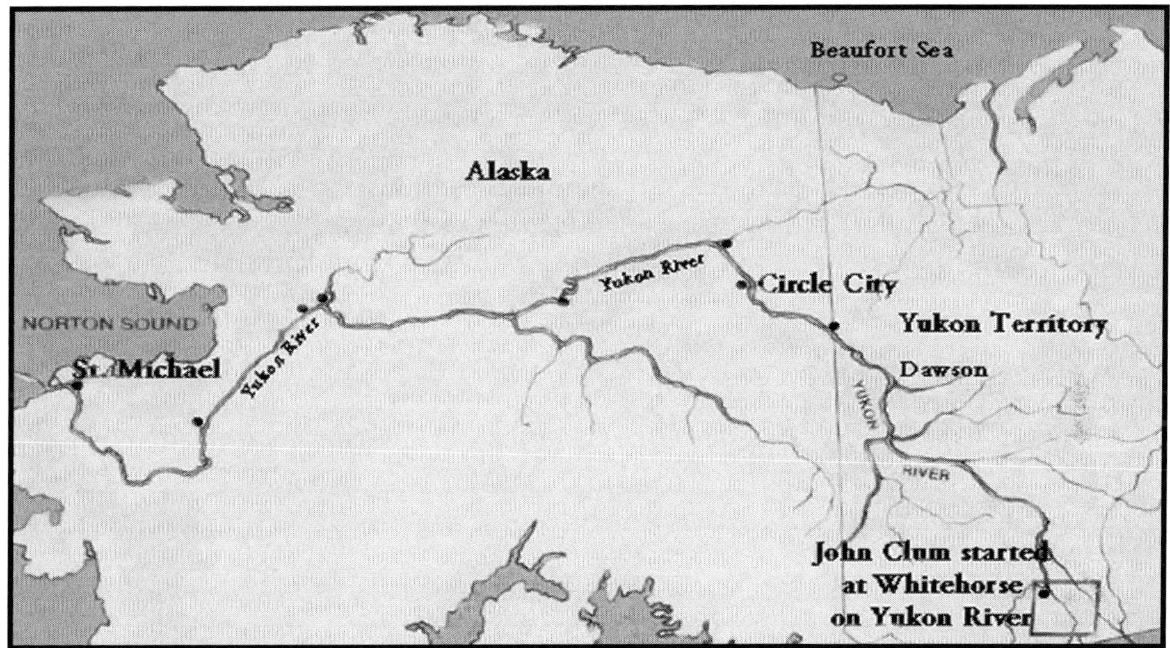

Mark the following settlements where John Clum founded new post offices in Cook Inlet and Prince William Sound, along with changing the name of Ounalaska in the Aleutians:
1) Unalaska 2) Seldovia 3) Homer 4) Sunrise 5) Tyonek 6) Orca

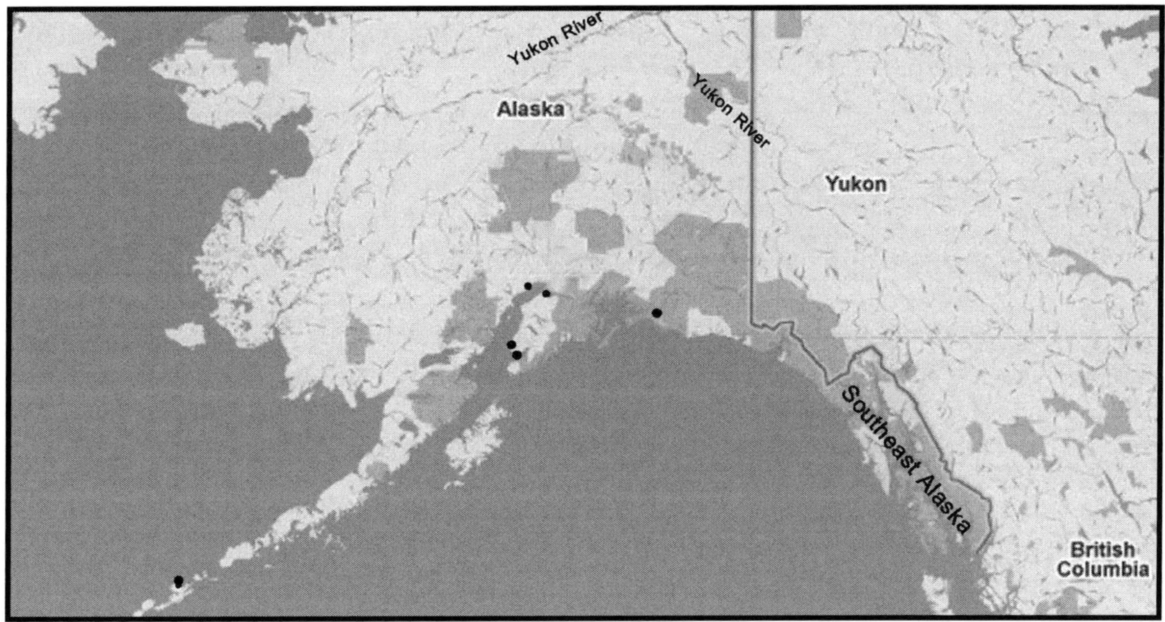

UNIT 4: ROUTES TO RESOURCES

LESSON 13: ALASKA'S PIONEERING POSTMEN

FACTS TO KNOW

Ben S. Downing – Developed the first mail route from Dawson to Nome
Fred Lockley – A mail carrier who started the first mail delivery service in Nome
Ben Taylor – Worked with Fred Lockley to start the first mail delivery service in Nome

COMPREHENSION QUESTIONS

1) Where was the first post office in Alaska under the U.S. government located? When was it established? ______________________________

____

____

2) What was mail communication like when Alaska was under Russian rule?

____

____

____

3) News of the Klondike Gold Rush in 1897 brought __________________ north from the Black Hills of South Dakota. He didn't mine for gold, however. Instead he set up the first mail route from ______________ to ______________.

4) _________________ was the largest general delivery address in the U.S. postal system the summer of 1900. In his book, "Alaska's First Free Mail Delivery in 1900," letter carrier ____________________________ noted that the _______________________ had to use five filing boxes just to sort letters for people named Johnson.

5) How did Fred Lockley and Ben Taylor come up with the idea to start the first free mail delivery service to businesses in Nome?

____

____

____

____

____

6) Name three challenges that the early postal carriers faced in Nome.

____

____

____

7) What are some of the ways that the post office attempted to transport the mail around Alaska? What modes of transport worked the best and why? ______________

____

____

____

DISCUSSION QUESTION

(Discuss this question with your teacher or write your answer in essay form below. Use additional paper if necessary.)

How did the people of Nome treat the postmen?

____

____

____

____

____

____

____

____

____

____

____

____

ENRICHMENT ACTIVITY

Imagine that you are a journalist for a newspaper in Nome, and you have been assigned to write a story about the first free mail delivery service in the territory. Write an article about the new service. Share details and quotes from the lesson, such as how the postmen were received by the people of Nome and the process that the mailmen received, sorted and delivered the mail.

LEARN MORE

Read more about Fred Lockley by visiting https://oregonencyclopedia.org/articles/lockley_fred_1871_1958_/#.WMC75zvyvIU

Clum's Post Offices

Word Search Puzzle

Find the words listed below

B	P	D	Z	G	J	U	M	K	E	O	I	A	H	U	K	V	T	W	F
O	Y	I	X	F	P	P	S	D	E	K	M	K	E	H	C	U	N	B	P
T	R	M	Y	S	A	I	V	O	D	L	E	S	K	E	R	A	E	W	U
D	A	C	E	O	N	C	Z	Y	A	W	G	A	K	S	X	Q	C	L	Z
K	M	N	A	M	H	O	U	M	P	K	R	L	H	R	L	H	S	K	K
Y	I	Y	V	Y	O	U	K	L	N	G	F	A	I	H	T	I	H	I	C
S	D	R	R	I	Z	N	L	U	T	O	F	N	U	C	O	Z	E	E	D
I	H	R	X	E	K	C	L	V	Y	K	A	U	W	U	A	X	E	S	K
V	A	Y	M	C	S	A	A	T	I	T	I	D	S	W	M	S	P	N	E
U	R	C	E	P	T	I	V	N	R	U	R	W	Y	P	Q	U	C	D	N
O	B	K	J	O	V	V	R	A	Y	A	B	O	E	S	V	T	A	U	O
L	O	T	U	R	F	Z	P	N	X	O	A	C	F	O	J	Q	M	N	Y
Z	R	F	U	E	Q	M	P	O	U	Y	N	N	Z	V	F	E	P	F	T
L	K	S	L	N	A	U	G	Y	P	S	K	O	N	Q	Q	U	E	E	V
J	Y	G	O	R	O	C	V	B	O	S	S	X	G	F	N	O	C	E	M
Z	A	Z	N	Z	S	T	M	I	C	H	A	E	L	P	D	H	U	P	X
E	F	D	M	H	D	I	I	N	A	Y	W	A	F	C	I	R	C	L	E
K	O	Y	U	K	U	K	Q	Z	I	H	O	M	E	R	G	A	O	I	X
A	M	E	S	M	K	T	W	I	U	H	P	R	R	A	T	S	N	Z	W
L	Q	A	P	G	F	W	W	O	T	J	F	I	M	X	M	Z	G	R	Q

SHEEP CAMP
CANYON
EAGLE
RAMPART
NULATO
NOME
SUNRISE
NUCHEK

PYRAMID HARBOR
DYEA
CIRCLE
WEARE
ANVIK
UNALASKA
HOMER
ORCA

STARR
SKAGWAY
FORT YUKON
KOYUKUK
ST MICHAEL
TYONEK
SELDOVIA
FAIRBANKS

UNIT 4: ROUTES TO RESOURCES

LESSON 14: THE TRAPPING LIFE

FACTS TO KNOW

Alaska Commercial Company – Held a monopoly on the fur trade
Trapper – A person who traps wild animals for fur, usually to sell or trade
Ed Ueeck – Alaskan trapper during the 1930s

COMPREHENSION QUESTIONS

1) The Athabascan people came to depend on many items brought north by the white men, including: ____

____

____

2) In addition to having a monopoly on the fur trade in Alaska, in what industries did the Alaska Commercial Company participate? ______________________

____

____

3) Established throughout Alaska, village stores became the center of all community activities. They served as the ______________________________

____.

4) Why did the Alaska Commercial Company change its name to the Northern Commercial Company in 1922? To where did the company headquarters relocate?

____

____

____

____

5) How did Ed Ueeck become a trapper? How many miles did he travel in an average day to check and reset traps? ______________________________

____

____

____

6) Describe the trapping life. ____

____

____

____

DISCUSSION QUESTION

(Discuss this question with your teacher or write your answer in essay form below. Use additional paper if necessary.)

Summarize what you learned about the trapping life from the diary of the "Wildman of Dry Bay."

____

____

____

____

____

____

____

____

____

____

____

____

____

____

____

ENRICHMENT ACTIVITY

Read more about the Athabaskan people by visiting the link below. Write a paragraph about what you learned.
http://www.akhistorycourse.org/alaskas-cultures/alaskas-heritage/chapter-2-3-athabaskans

LEARN MORE

Read more about early trapping and the fur trade by visiting http://www.akhistorycourse.org/americas-territory/alaskas-heritage/chapter-4-14-trading-and-trapping

Natives Trade Furs for Western Goods

Word Scramble

Unscramble the words below

1. onctot rcifab	________	A light-weight material from which clothes are made.
2. prugdwoen	________	An explosive consisting of a powdered mixture of saltpeter, sulfur and charcoal.
3. bsnealtk	________	Large pieces of woolen or similar material used to cover beds or other coverings for warmth.
4. augrs	________	A sweet crystalline substance obtained from various plants.
5. bsmoc	________	Strips of plastic, metal or wood with rows of narrow teeth, used for untangling or arranging the hair.
6. poas	________	A substance used with water for washing and cleaning.
7. rlofu	________	A powder obtained by grinding grain, typically wheat, and used to make bread, cakes and pastry.
8. tbaococ	________	Nicotine-rich leaves of an American plant, which are cured by a process of drying and fermentation for smoking or chewing.
9. vnesik	________	Sharp blades attached to handles that are used for cutting or as a weapon.
10. stletke	________	Vessels, usually made of metal and with a handle, used for boiling liquids or cooking foods.

UNIT 4: ROUTES TO RESOURCES

LESSON 15: DALTON TURNS TIMBER INTO GOLD

FACTS TO KNOW

Jack Dalton – He established a toll road and built a sawmill in Southeast Alaska
Tlingit Indians – Indigenous people of Southeast Alaska
Sawmill – A facility where logs are cut into timber

COMPREHENSION QUESTIONS

1) Jack Dalton established a ______________________ from Pyramid Harbor on the Lynn Canal to the ____________ River, on which around 2,000 ________________ had traveled and made a welcome addition to many miner's food supply during the ______________ Gold Rush. His trail would later become part of the ________________________.

2) How did the Tlingit Indians utilize timber? How did they profit from timber when non-Native settlers came to the territory? ____________________________________

____

____

____

____

3) How did Jack Dalton profit from timber in 1899? ________________________

____

____

____

____

4) Where did the lumber come from for major building projects in Alaska, such as Fort Seward in Haines? ____

____

____

____

____

DISCUSSION QUESTION

(Discuss this question with your teacher or write your answer in essay form below. Use additional paper if necessary.)

The Tlingit people and Jack Dalton understood that timber was an important resource that many people needed. What are some things that we use timber for today?

ENRICHMENT ACTIVITY

Watch this five-minute video to see an aerial view of a modern-day sawmill in Washington by visiting https://www.youtube.com/watch?v=NvbgwdTGoyo&t=35s

LEARN MORE

Read more about the lumber industry in Alaska by visiting http://www.akhistorycourse.org/americas-territory/alaskas-heritage/chapter-4-17-farming-herding-and-lumbering

UNIT 4: ROUTES TO RESOURCES

LESSON 16: ROUTES TO GOLD, COPPER AND COAL

FACTS TO KNOW

E.J. Glave – English explorer and traveling companion of Jack Dalton
Matanuska River – 75-mile-long river in Southcentral Alaska

COMPREHENSION QUESTIONS

1) How did E.J. Glave describe Jack Dalton? ______________________________

2) Describe the disagreement between Jack Dalton and the railway company. ________

3) How was the disagreement in the question above resolved? __________________

4) What task did federal Bureau of Mines director A.M. Holmes give Jack Dalton in 1913?

5) What was Jack Dalton's solution to this problem? _______________________

DISCUSSION QUESTION

(Discuss this question with your teacher or write your answer in essay form below. Use additional paper if necessary.)

Jack Dalton was a man that solved the problems that he saw around him. Name another person in history that became famous by solving a problem. Discuss the problem and how this person solved it.

ENRICHMENT ACTIVITY

Read more about Jack Dalton and others who established road transportation in early Alaska by visiting the link below. Take notes and share what you learned orally with the class.

http://www.akhistorycourse.org/americas-territory/alaskas-heritage/chapter-4-10-road-transportation

TIME TO REVIEW

Review Chapters 12-16 of your book before moving on the Unit Review. See how many questions you can answer without looking at your book.

Routes to Resources

Crossword Puzzle

Read Across and Down clues and fill in blank boxes that match numbers on the clues

Across

3 This man's ability to deal with Alaska Natives proved invaluable
4 Small enclosure where trappers kept their food
6 Address used when sending mail if one does not know the exact address of an individual
9 Another name for a postman
13 Business that Jack Dalton built in 1899 that produced 5,000 board feet of lumber a day
16 Jack Dalton definitely was one of these
17 Place where Dalton established his headquarters for coal transportation project
18 Route that trappers followed to trap furbearers
19 These animals were too hard to harness break for mail deliveries
20 Natives sold these foot coverings to stampeders
22 The one battle Dalton did not win involved this mode of transportation
24 Town that was the largest general delivery address in the United States in 1900
28 In the 1920s, these spelled the end to dog teams delivering mail in Alaska
29 These people sold 75,000 pelts to traders in 1880
31 A sawmill, which was the first business built, owned and operated by Natives in Alaska, was at this location
32 This was piled 10-20 feet high along Nome's waterfront in 1900
36 Type of boats that Alaska Natives made from timber in Southeast Alaska
38 Dalton went to this city to get men, supplies and horses for the Matanuska Valley coal transportation project
39 What postmen deliver
40 What one puts on mail to show the postage has been paid to send it

Down

1 Mailman Ben Downing would get angry if one of these was stolen from a shelter
2 This adventurer, who became a trader, was convinced that gold extended from the Yukon into Alaska
3 How Ben Downing delivered mail
5 Deep snow proved too much for these animals to carry the mail
7 Method Russians used to send mail
8 Battleship that tested the Matanuska Valley coal
10 When trapping season ended
11 Dalton figured out how to get this valuable resource from the Matanuska Valley down to tidewater
12 This activity drove economic activity following America's purchase of Alaska
14 Type of tool used to catch furbearing animals
15 Unusual place that many miners gave in order to get their mail delivered
21 Quality coal deposits from this area met U.S. Navy requirements
23 Boats that carried freight from steamships to the beach of Nome
25 Prefering to use spruce for these, Alaska Natives took these apart and made tools
26 These were built about 25 miles apart on a mail route

Routes to Resources

Crossword Puzzle

Down (Continued)

27 Mail carrier from Oregon who traveled to Alaska when gold was discovered at Nome

30 About 2,000 of this type of animal crossed Jack Dalton's toll road during the Klondike Gold Rush era

33 Jack Dalton and this man decided to solve the "defective transportation" problem in Alaska

34 What mail is carried in for delivery

35 Editor of the *Tombstone Epitaph* who became the post office inspector for Alaska in 1898

37 Man who started out harvesting crops and then became a trapper between Nelchina and Matanuska rivers

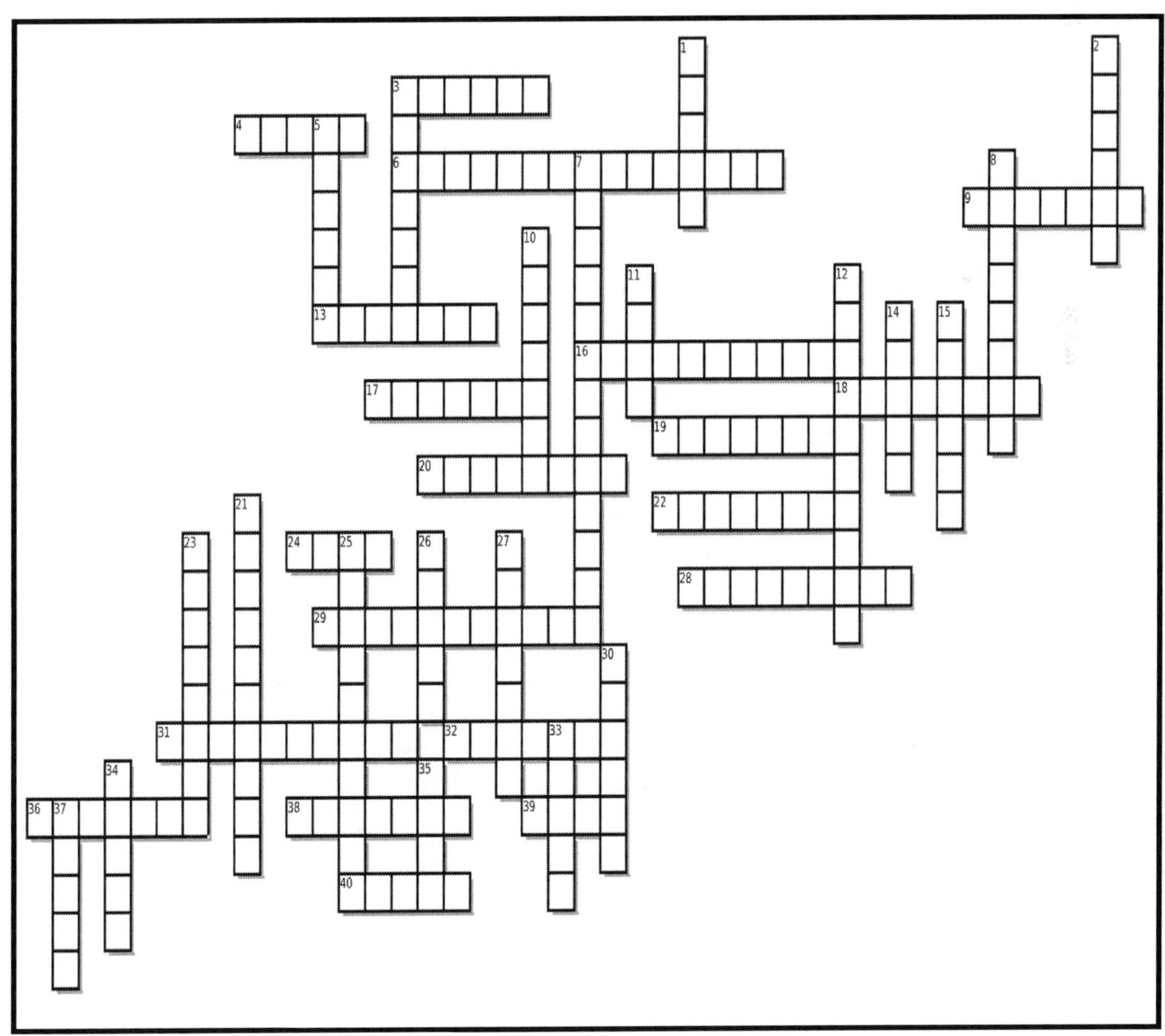

Courtesy Alaska State Library

Above: Dalton Transportation Company did a good business hauling supplies across the White Pass Trail during the Klondike Gold Rush. Sometimes Jack Dalton used oxen to pull loaded sleds, as seen in this photograph taken on April 2, 1899.

Below: U.S. President Warren G. Harding, seen here seated on a bear skin on the steps of the government coal mine in Chickaloon, visited Alaska to help celebrate the completion of the Alaska Railroad in 1923. The coal mine had shut down the year before his visit.

Courtesy Alaska State Library

UNIT 4: ROUTES TO RESOURCES

REVIEW LESSONS 12-16

Write down what you remember about:

John Clum ______________________________

____

Ben S. Downing ______________________________

____

Fred Lockley ______________________________

____

Ben Taylor ______________________________

____

Alaska Commercial Company ______________________________

____

Trapper ______________________________

____

Ed Ueeck ______________________________

____

Jack Dalton ______________________________

____

Tlingit Indians ______________________________

____

Sawmill ______________________________

____

E.J. Glave ______________________________

____

Matanuska River ______________________________

____

Fill in the blanks:

1) The colorful ________________ of the famous *Tombstone Epitaph* made his mark on Alaska in the late _________. ___________________ also became the first mayor of ______________________, and it was during this era that the legendary gunfight at the OK Corral was fought.

2) But it was another one of ________________ ventures that brought him to Alaska and gave him the opportunity to leave his mark on the new land. In March 1898, he was appointed ________________________ for the territory.

3) As ______________________________, _________________ set up post offices in Southeast Alaska, along the ___________________________ and then down to the ______________________________, where he changed the name of the post office at Ounalaska to _________________________.

4) ____________________________ came north from the Black Hills of South Dakota following the discovery of ________ in the Klondike. He took the job of creating the first mail route from ___________ to ______________.

5) It was while ______________________ and his friend _________________________ were standing in a more than block-long line at the post office that he conceived the idea of ______________________________ to businesses in _________________. _________________, the post office inspector, wrote up the letter authorizing the plan and sent _______________ and _______________________ on their way.

6) Sometimes postmen spent up to _________ hours ______________, _______________ and ________________ the massive amount of mail when several ______________ unloaded simultaneously. But the mail didn't just arrive by _________. It also came by ___________________ from places like Dawson.

7) Postal employees' normal schedules involved from _______ to ________ hours per day. The dedicated mailmen also had to contend with patrons' frequent ________________ in the hustle and bustle of gold-rush Nome.

8) With the gold rushes came the first attempt to introduce _______________ as beasts of burden in the new land of ice and snow, but ____________________ proved too much of a handicap. Next, ______________ and ______________ were tried. The _________________ proved intractable and impossible to harness break, so it was up to the _________. In Interior Alaska, the ____________________ was the first mode of transportation to prove successful in carrying the mail – until the ________________ came along.

9) Trapping worked out well for many families because they could live their ______________________________ in the summer months. After the first hard freeze, they set _________________________. The winter routine meant checking the _______________, returning to the cabin to _______________ the animals, ____________________ the fur and then head out again to ____________________ traps. Most families traveled by ____________________ back to their villages to spend the Christmas holidays, ___________their furs and purchase more ________________ for the rest of the winter.

10) After establishing the first ________________ in the territory, ______________________ had an area around the Porcupine gold field surveyed – 36 miles from Haines up the Chilkat Valley – he realized that more gold lay in the ______________________________ surrounding the town site. He built a __________________ in 1899 that produced 5,000 ____________________________________a day.

11) Jack Dalton's traveling partner, _______________________, wrote this about him: "Dalton is a most desirable partner – has ___________________________, cool and deliberate in times of danger and possessed _________________________ in dealing with the ______________ … as a camp cook, I've never seen his equal."

12) _______________, _______________ then _____________ challenged Dalton's trailblazing talents. Some thought that the _____________ deposits at Chickaloon in the ______________________ Valley might meet the U.S. Navy's requirements.

13) Along with federal ________________________ director A.M. Holmes, Dalton went to look the mine over in the year _________. Dalton received the task __________________ ____– at a cost the agency could afford.

14) Dalton successfully transported _______________ from the _____________________ ____________________ to tidewater to be used by the U.S. Navy. After the ice went out of the Inlet, the coal was placed aboard the battleship _______________________________ for testing. But before anything could be done about providing a regular supply of ______________ ,the Navy converted to _______________.

UNIT 4: ROUTES TO RESOURCES

UNIT TEST

Choose *two* of the following questions to answer in paragraph form. Use as much detail as possible to completely answer the question. Use extra paper in back of the book if needed.

1) Who was John Clum? Name two of his ventures. What venture brought him to Alaska? Was his job in Alaska easy or hard? Explain your answer.

2) Describe how the first free postal delivery service in Nome started. Who started it? How did he come up with the idea? What need did he see in Nome?

3) What is a trapper? Why was trapping an important business in early Alaska? Briefly describe what a year for a trapping family was like in early Alaska.

4) Describe Jack Dalton. Name two ventures for which Jack Dalton was famous. Explain how he got involved in each venture.

UNIT 4: ROUTES TO RESOURCES

Review Questions ______ (possible 12 pts.)
Fill-the-Blanks ______ (possible 14 pts.)

Unit Test

Essay 1
Demonstrates understanding of the topic ______ (possible 5 pts.)
Answered the questions completely and accurately ______ (possible 5 pts.)
Composition is neat ______ (possible 5 pts.)
Grammar and Spelling ______ (possible 5 pts.)

Essay 2
Demonstrates understanding of the topic ______ (possible 5 pts.)
Answered the questions completely and accurately ______ (possible 5 pts.)
Composition is neat ______ (possible 5 pts.)
Grammar and Spelling ______ (possible 5 pts.)

Subtotal Points ______ (possible 66 pts.)

Extra Credit
Word Puzzle ______ (5 pt. per completed puzzle)
Complete an Enrichment Activity ______ (possible 5 pts.)
Oral presentation ______ (possible 10 pts.)

Total Extra Credit ______

Total Unit Points ______

GRADE CHART

A 58-66+ points

B 51-57 points

C 44-50 points

D 37-43 points

UNIT 5: PRINCE WILLIAM SOUND

LESSON 17: GLACIER TRAIL BIRTHS VALDEZ

FACTS TO KNOW

Valdez Glacier Trail – A trail along the Valdez Glacier that many stampeders traveled to find gold along the Copper River
Copper Center – A settlement at the confluence of the Klutina and Copper rivers
Scurvy – A disease resulting from lack of vitamin C; often from lack of fruits and vegetables in one's diet
Port Valdez – Gold seekers formed a tent city here in 1898

COMPREHENSION QUESTIONS

1) According to the authors of *Valdez Gold Rush Trails of 1898-99*, what was one of the greatest hoaxes in Alaska's history? Why did they call it a hoax?

____

____

____

____

2) What kind of conditions did prospectors find while traveling the Valdez Glacier Trail?

____

____

____

____

3) Not all the thousands of prospectors that crossed the glacial trail were men. Name one of the women who made it across the trail. What did she do after she crossed the trail?

____

____

____

____

____

____

4) Why was there a scurvy epidemic in Copper City during the winter of 1898-1899?

____

____

____

5) When was Port Valdez established? To whom did the area belong before the European explorers arrived? ____

____

DISCUSSION QUESTION

(Discuss this question with your teacher or write your answer in essay form below. Use additional paper if necessary.)

Think about all the gold rush cities that we have studied in this book so far (and in Volume 1, if you read it). Do you see any similarities in the impact the gold rush had on these cities? What seemed to happen to the cities when the gold rush ended in those locations?

____

____

____

____

____

____

____

____

____

____

____

____

____

____

____

ENRICHMENT ACTIVITY

Imagine that you are a medical professional in Alaska during the gold rush period. You are tired of treating so many scurvy patients, so you decide to create a flyer to educate stampeders about what scurvy is and how to prevent it. Create your flyer using information from the lesson and any additional resources.

You can read more about symptoms of scurvy, what it is and how to prevent it by visiting http://www.bbc.co.uk/history/british/empire_seapower/captaincook_scurvy_01.shtml

LEARN MORE

Read more about early Alaska railroads in Valdez, Cordova and other areas by visiting http://www.akhistorycourse.org/americas-territory/alaskas-heritage/chapter-4-11-railroad-transportation

UNIT 5: PRINCE WILLIAM SOUND

LESSON 18: CORDOVA – A TOWN BORN OF STRIFE

FACTS TO KNOW

Cordova – A small town located near the Copper River
Michael J. Heney – Irish railroad contractor who thought that Cordova would be a good spot for a railroad
Guggenheim-Morgan Syndicate – Companies that partnered and attempted to monopolize the coal resources in Alaska

COMPREHENSION QUESTIONS

1) Why was it important to have a railroad through Cordova? What did Michael Heney discover when he surveyed the railway route? ______________________________

____

____

____

2) What obstacles were in the way of building the railroad over Michael Heney's route?

____

____

____

____

3) What was early Cordova like? ______________________________________

____

____

____

4) What happened in 1907 when the Valdez railroad men attempted to break down the Guggenheim-Morgan Syndicate's rock barricade at Keystone Canyon? ____________

____

____

____

5) How did the incident at Keystone Canyon eventually lead to the end of the syndicate's ability to monopolize coal resources in Alaska? ______________________________

____

____

6) Why did 300 residents of Cordova march to the Alaska Steamship Company dock in 1911? Did the marchers get the result that they wanted? ______________________________

____

____

____

____

DISCUSSION QUESTION

(Discuss this question with your teacher or write your answer in essay form below. Use additional paper if necessary.)

Compare what you know about the Cordova Coal Party and the Boston Tea Party. What are some similarities? What are some differences?

____

____

____

____

____

____

____

____

____

____

____

____

____

____

____

LEARN MORE

Read more about the fight for railroads by visiting http://www.akhistorycourse.org/south-central-alaska/1900-1915-fight-for-a-railroad

MAP ACTIVITY

Find these on the map below: 1) Port Valdez 2) Cordova 3) Copper River 4) Keystone Canyon

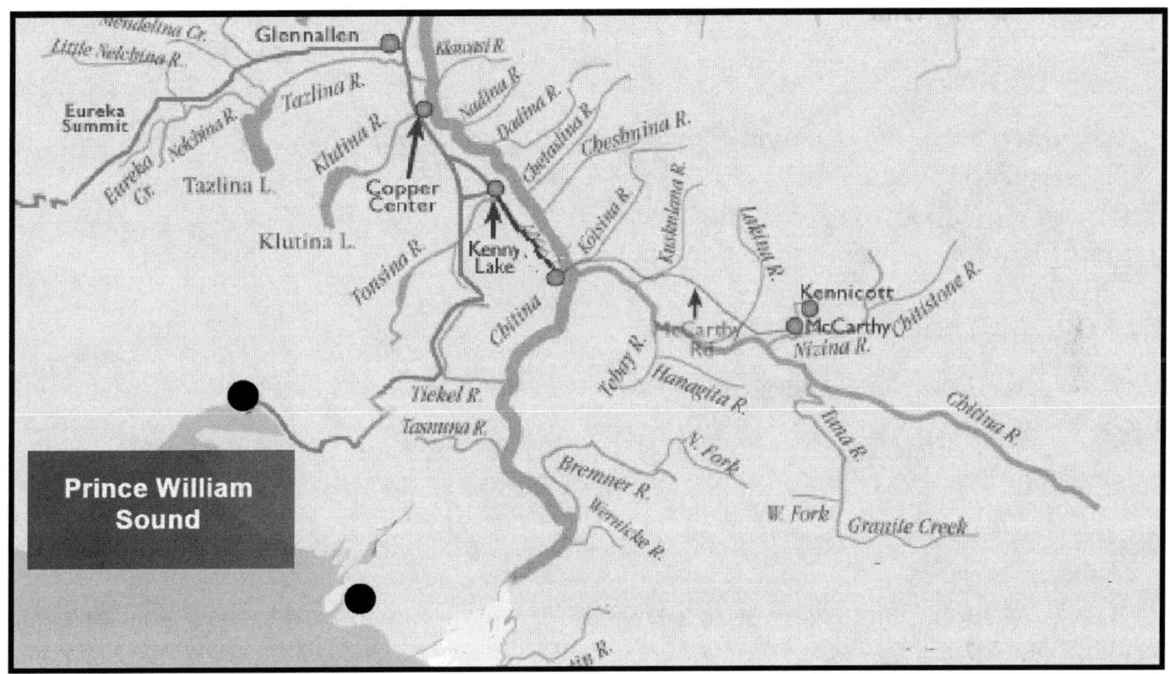

UNIT 5: PRINCE WILLIAM SOUND

LESSON 19: SEWARD'S RESURRECTIONS

FACTS TO KNOW

Alexander Baranof – Russian explorer who named (Voskresenskaya Gavan) Resurrection Bay in 1792
Seward – Small town named after Secretary of State William H. Seward
John Ballaine – Founder of the town of Seward

COMPREHENSION QUESTIONS

1) What led Alexander Baranof to Resurrection Bay? Why did he name it Resurrection Bay? ______________________________

2) Why did John Ballaine want to name the town of Seward after Secretary of State William H. Seward? ______________________________

3) What issue did the postal inspector have with naming the town Seward? How did John Ballaine resolve this matter? ______________________________

4) How did Seward go from a booming construction town in 1903 to a town waiting for resurrection within a decade? ______________________________

5) What happened in 1914 to resurrect the town? ______________________________
____
____
____

DISCUSSION QUESTION

(Discuss this question with your teacher or write your answer in essay form below. Use additional paper if necessary.)

Do you know the story behind the name of your hometown? Was it named after a special person? If you don't know, do a little research at your local library or online.

____
____
____
____
____
____
____
____
____
____
____
____
____
____
____

LEARN MORE

Look for this book at your local library:
The Copper Spike, Lone E. Janson. Anchorage: Alaska Northwest Publishing Company, 1975.

TIME TO REVIEW

Review Chapters 17-19 of your book before moving on the Unit Review. See how many questions you can answer without looking at your book.

Prince William Sound Develops

Word Scramble Puzzle

Unscramble the words below

	Scrambled	Answer	Clue
1.	dlevaz		A glacier birthed this town as it grew into a supply center in late 1890s
2.	hrdsnrcaio		The Keystone Canyon Trail eventually became this highway
3.	ghcchua		Historically the territory south of Valdez belongs to these people
4.	ahtna		Historically the territory north of Valdez belongs to these people
5.	lcsumi		Fort first located three miles from the head of Valdez Bay
6.	oradasrli		Companies building these caused considerable turmoil in Prince William Sound in the early 1900s
7.	ydolrnse		The man who convinced investors to support the Alaska Home Railroad, which left people with no jobs and little money when it flopped
8.	peopcr		A mountain of this was found in the Wrangell Mountains in the early 1900s
9.	voocard		Town born when engineers chose its location to be the terminus of a railroad to carry precious ore from the Kennecott mines
10.	yehen		Irish contractor who surveyed a railroad route through glaciers

Prince William Sound Develops

Word Scramble Puzzle

Continued

11. farbaon	______	Man who named Resurrection Bay
12. lonilmi olardl	______	Name of bridge at the glaciers along the route of the Copper River and Northwestern Railway
13. latalka	______	Town in the heart of oil and coalfields 40 miles east of Cordova
14. cdnetaysi	______	The Guggenheim/Morgan companies, which owned copper and coal mines near Cordova, are one of these
15. thopnci	______	First director of the U.S. Forest Service who ordered the withdrawal of vast coalfield
16. adrswe	______	This town on Resurrection Bay started out in 1902 from a plan to build a railroad
17. lenaialb	______	Man who chose the name for Seward
18. ausitvk	______	The first name of the town that became Seward
19. seeoltvor	______	U.S. President who gave approval to the name Seward
20. asalak cnrtale	______	Railroad in Seward that went bankrupt in 1908

UNIT 5: PRINCE WILLIAM SOUND

REVIEW LESSONS 17-19

Write down what you remember about:

Valdez Glacier Trail ______________________________

____

Copper Center ______________________________

____

Scurvy ______________________________

____

Port Valdez ______________________________

____

Cordova ______________________________

____

Michael J. Heney ______________________________

____

Guggenheim-Morgan Syndicate ______________________________

____

Alexander Baranof ______________________________

____

Seward ______________________________

____

John Ballaine ______________________________

____

Fill in the blanks:

1) "Gold in Alaska!" "________________ – Best Trail!" rang the headlines in ________________. Promoters of this route claimed that prospectors would find more gold in the ________________ soil along the ____________ River than they would in the Canadian ______________. And that was one of the greatest ___________ in Alaska's history, according to Jim and Nancy Lethcoe in their book, "*Valdez Gold Rush Trails of 1898-99*."

2) Some stampeders who made it over the glacier stayed in Port ___________, named in 1790 by Don Salvador Fidalgo. Salvador also named ____________, Port ____________ and other spots while on his voyage to Alaska to investigate the extent of Russian involvement and to reestablish _________________ claim to the area.

3) The shooting of a _____________ railroad worker on a barricaded track in ______________ Canyon on September 25, _________, resulted in payoffs, perjury and manipulation by the ___________________________ Syndicate and ended the syndicate's attempt to control ____________ resources in Alaska

4) Many Alaskans' dreams of riches from ________ and ________ dried up when Pinchot ordered the withdrawal of those coalfield holdings to protect them from the ______________________Syndicate. Communities had to start importing ________ from ______________, and many Alaskans resented being forced to purchase high-dollar _________ from foreigners when Alaska had an abundance of the resource.

5) Shovels in hand, 300 __________________ marched down to the Alaska Steamship Company dock in 1911. They formed the ____________________, and shouted "Give us Alaska coal," as several tons of ___________________ were dumped into the bay.

6) Russian explorer ______________________ named __________________ Bay in 1792.

7) Founder _______________________ was convinced the city of ______________ would one day be the metropolis of a great territory and should fittingly bear the name of the man who foresaw the primacy of the Pacific Ocean in the world's future, Secretary of State ___________________________.

8) _______________ became a roaring construction town, but the boom collapsed when the "powers that be" in Washington decided to conserve Alaska ________. The _________________________ went bankrupt in 1908, but re-emerged as the ______________________________ in 1910.

9) At no time was the railroad even able to earn _____________________. Its tracks, bridges and docks were not adequately maintained, and by __________ it was hardly in operating condition. ____________ soon became a town waiting for a ______________.

10) The U.S. government had chosen ____________________ as the saltwater terminus for its proposed ___________________________. The boom was on again. From the states arrived boatloads of men seeking work on ______________________________.

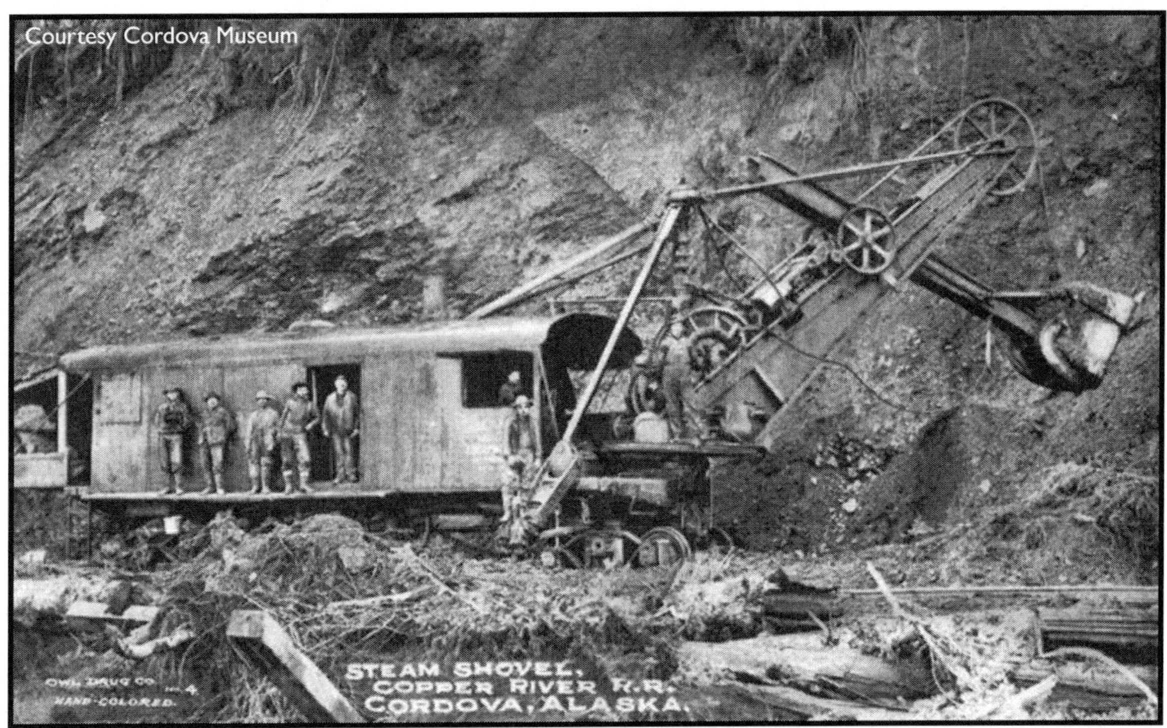

Men and machines, like the steam shovel above, worked hard to get copper and coal out of the mountains in Alaska. They also worked tirelessly to build the community of Cordova, seen below. This photo shows First Avenue in 1909.

UNIT 5: PRINCE WILLIAM SOUND

UNIT TEST

Choose *two* of the following questions to answer in paragraph form. Use as much detail as possible to completely answer the question. Use extra paper in back of the book if needed.

1) Why was the promotion of the Valdez Glacier Trail called one of the biggest hoaxes in Alaska's history? What kind of conditions did prospectors find when they got there? What city was formed as a result of the thousands of stampeders that came to cross the glacier?

2) How did the Guggenheim-Morgan Syndicate attempt to monopolize coal resources in Alaska? What happened at Keystone Canyon in 1907? How did this eventually result in ruining Guggenheim-Morgan Syndicate's plan to monopolize coal in Alaska?

3) Explain why railroad transportation was important in Alaska during the early 1900s. What were some of the obstacles that the railroad companies had to face in order to build the railroads?

4) Describe the town of Seward. Who founded it? Who was the town named after and why? Why did the town need a resurrection in 1914? What happened to cause a second boom in 1914?

UNIT 5: PRINCE WILLIAM SOUND

Review Questions ______ (possible 10 pts.)
Fill-the-Blanks ______ (possible 10 pts.)

Unit Test

Essay 1

Demonstrates understanding of the topic ______ (possible 5 pts.)
Answered the questions completely and accurately ______ (possible 5 pts.)
Composition is neat ______ (possible 5 pts.)
Grammar and Spelling ______ (possible 5 pts.)

Essay 2

Demonstrates understanding of the topic ______ (possible 5 pts.)
Answered the questions completely and accurately ______ (possible 5 pts.)
Composition is neat ______ (possible 5 pts.)
Grammar and Spelling ______ (possible 5 pts.)

Subtotal Points ______ (possible 60 pts.)

Extra Credit

Word Puzzle ______ (5 pt. per completed puzzle)
Complete an Enrichment Activity ______ (possible 5 pts.)
Oral presentation ______ (possible 10 pts.)

Total Extra Credit ______

Total Unit Points ______

GRADE CHART

A 54-60+ points

B 48-53 points

C 42-47 points

D 36-41 points

UNIT 6: WILDERNESS TRAILS

LESSON 20: SLED DOGS LEAD THE WAY
LESSON 21: BLAZING THE IDITAROD TRAIL

Note: Read both chapters 20 and 21 before completing this lesson.

FACTS TO KNOW

Sled dog team – A group of dogs trained to pull a sled for travel
Lead dog – The dog that leads the sled dog team
Iditarod Trail – The approximately 1,000-mile route from Seward to Nome
Walter Goodwin – Hired by the Alaska Road Commission to scout a trail from Seward to Nome

COMPREHENSION QUESTIONS

1) In what ways did Native Alaskans utilize sled dogs during the 1700-1800s?

____
____
____
____

2) How did the Russian Explorers improve upon the sled dog system?

____
____
____
____

3) Why were sled dogs in even greater demand during the late 1890s and early 1900s?

____
____
____
____

4) How did Iditarod become the largest town in Alaska for a brief period in the early 1900s? ______________________________

____
____
____

5) What trail did Walter Goodwin establish in 1911? Why was this trail important?

____

____

____

6) Who was Jujiro Wada? What did the city of Seward hire him to do?

____

____

____

DISCUSSION QUESTION

(Discuss this question with your teacher or write your answer in essay form below. Use additional paper if necessary.)

What do you think it was like for early Russian settlers in Alaska to begin traveling by sled dog teams?

____

____

____

____

____

____

____

____

____

____

____

____

____

____

ENRICHMENT ACTIVITY

Learn more about sled dogs by watching this short YouTube video:
https://www.youtube.com/watch?v=6nVfFNbxX7s

LEARN MORE

Look for this book at your local library:
Everything I Know About Training and Racing Sled Dogs, George Attla. Rome, New York: Arner Publications, 1974.

UNIT 6: WILDERNESS TRAILS

LESSON 22: IDITAROD TRAIL PHOTO ESSAY

Fill in the blanks:

1) ________________ have a long and illustrious past in the Great North. Natives bred ________, which became part of Alaskan families' everyday lives, for survival in the harsh climate. Two breeds were most common: ________________________________.

2) The large ______________ mostly were used for pulling heavy loads of ________________________ between camps and villages. ____________________ were exported to Alaska during the gold-rush era and used for transportation of ________________________.

3) The town of ___________________________ grew out of the wilderness after prospectors ____________________ and ____________________discovered gold along the _________________________ River, a tributary of the Innoko, in December 1908.

4) A _____________ team pulled into ______________ on Dec. 23, 1910, carrying one-half ton of gold dust, valued at $210,000, from the ______________ gold fields. Consigned to Brown and Hawkins, it was the largest gold dust shipment ever carried by ________ team in Alaska.

5) The blazing of the _____________Trail opened a new route to transport the precious gold from _____________ to _______________. ____________________ popped up along the _______________Trail before more substantial structures were built.

ENRICHMENT ACTIVITY

Choose one or two pictures from the lesson, and write your own paragraph about each picture. Make up your own story about what is going on in the picture.

LEARN MORE

Look for this article at your local library:
"Is Alaska Mining an Endangered Industry?" by Chuck Hawley in THE ALASKA JOURNAL 9 (3) (Summer 1979): 14-23

MAP ACTIVITY

Trace the Iditarod Trail from Seward to Nome on the map below. Mark on the map the following spots that the lesson mentions along the trail:

1) Seward 2) Girdwood 3) Knik 4) Susitna 5) Skwentna 6) Takotna
7) Iditarod 8) Dishkakat 9) Kaltag 10) Unalakleet 11) Nome

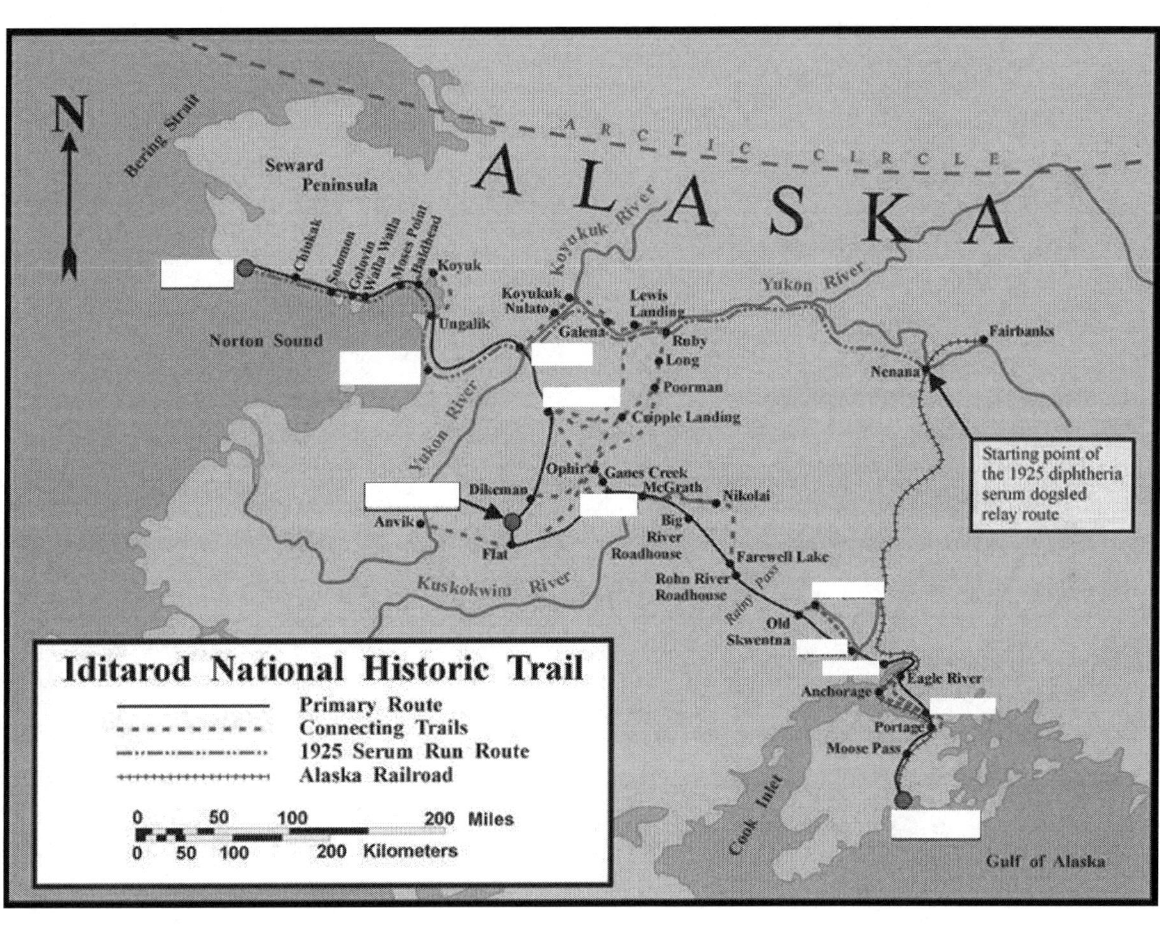

Places Along the Iditarod Trail

Word Search Puzzle

Find the words on the list below

```
W A Z X M A N T O K A T P E K L U T N A
J N C Z H L N E Z A F N D W N Z O W M L
O T R P K G T E W R N N I E Y Z B E Y L
L N N H B A Z Y E V F T K A E M U V O T
W E U N A L A K L E E T E K V H K H K D
L W K A L T A G X W Y X M E E W J B O C
D K K A U I B E D K Y K A G K W Z A N B
O S V X I W Q O M R A S N F M L Q B N T
N N C A X T O I E O Q S Z P N L A E I J
I G R U C W P V H N N A R E T X V T N J
V M A F D R O I S J D P D N M U U W H H
O M R R O C T U D S Z Y A D W X B L D D
L C I K S C N N M I R N Z D Z X K N I K
O G D I L D L B U O T I X U P U G U S G
G R D C N O I T A T S A N T I S U S H S
A A I I R B H R J A R R R B Z O T E K I
W T U H L A I T Q L U N Y O U T V D A O
G H V I B H A Z L U B A E B D T T D K U
D V Z S P L F F A N Y N D V X E M L A U
W I O O F F Y S E W A R D Y K R K Y T D
```

SEWARD	SUSITNA STATION	TALKEETNA
INNOKO	KALTAG	NULATO
OPHIR	TAKOTNA	MCGRATH
NOME	GIRDWOOD	EKLUTNA
KNIK	SKWENTNA	RAINY PASS
DISHKAKAT	UNALAKLEET	GOLOVIN
IDITAROD	FLAT	DISCOVERY
OTTER	DIKEMAN	RUBY

UNIT 7: A FEW TRAILBLAZERS

LESSON 23: BEACONS IN THE WILDERNESS

FACTS TO KNOW

Tributary – A stream that flows into a larger stream or lake
Arthur Harper – One of three early pioneers who set up strategic supply posts along the Yukon
Jack McQuesten – One of three early piöneers who set up strategic supply posts along the Yukon
Alfred Mayo – One of three early pioneers who set up strategic supply posts along the Yukon River

COMPREHENSION QUESTIONS

1) What led Jack McQuesten to the Yukon? ______________________________
____
____
____

2) What early pioneers did McQuesten meet up with on his way to Fort Yukon? ______
____
____
____

3) Why were Russian explorers, the Hudson Bay Company and Alaska Commercial Company uninterested in gold? ______________________________
____
____
____

4) What did the men learn when they attempted to obtain information about the tributaries of the Yukon River? How did Jack McQuesten and Arthur Harper make a living in the Yukon? ______________________________
____
____
____

5) What important contribution did Jack McQuesten, Arthur Harper and Al Mayo make to the Yukon gold rush? ____

____

____

DISCUSSION QUESTION

(Discuss this question with your teacher or write your answer in essay form below. Use additional paper if necessary.)

Jack McQuesten, Arthur Harper and Al Mayo never became rich from their famous work in the Yukon. What do you think this trio gained by their work?

____

____

____

____

____

____

____

____

____

____

____

____

____

____

ENRICHMENT ACTIVITY

Spend some time reading the Website for the Alaska Mining Hall of Fame at http://alaskamininghalloffame.org. See how many names you recognize from your study of Alaska mining history on the Inductees page.

LEARN MORE

Read more about Al Mayo by visiting http://alaskamininghalloffame.org/inductees/mayo.php

UNIT 7: A FEW TRAILBLAZERS

LESSON 24: VOICE OF THE YUKON

FACTS TO KNOW

Robert Service – A famous English poet who wrote about life in the North
Whitehorse – The capital city of the Yukon that inspired Robert Service to write his first poems

COMPREHENSION QUESTIONS

1) Famous humorist Will Rogers, who was proud to be a "______________ man," said that Robert Service served the _____________ man "__________________________ well seasoned with plenty of calories and tasty trimmings!" Many of Service's poems were inspired by the __________________of the gold rush.

2) Where was Robert Service born? Where did he live most of his life? Why have Alaskans "adopted" him? ____
____
____
____

3) How did Robert Service end up in Canada? What did he do for a living before he began writing poetry? ____
____
____
____

4) What led Robert Service to begin writing poetry? ____________________________
____
____
____

5) What was the title of the first book published by Robert Service? What are some topics that Robert Service wrote about in his poetry? ___________________________
____
____
____

6) Name two of Robert Service's famous poems or books. How many poems did he say he wrote? What was his goal? ____

____

____

DISCUSSION QUESTION

(Discuss this question with your teacher or write your answer in essay form below. Use additional paper if necessary.)

Why were many Robert Service fans surprised when they met him? How was his demeanor different from his poetry?

____

____

____

____

____

____

____

____

____

____

____

____

____

____

ENRICHMENT ACTIVITY

Spend some time in nature with a notebook and pen like Robert Service. See if you can write your own poem about what you see, smell, hear or touch. Don't worry about making it perfect. Enjoy the creative process.

LEARN MORE

Read more about Robert Service and his poetry by visiting https://www.poetryfoundation.org/poems-and-poets/poets/detail/robert-w-service

UNIT 7: A FEW TRAILBLAZERS

LESSON 25: SOURDOUGH PREACHER PAINTER

FACTS TO KNOW

Eustace Paul Ziegler – Missionary to Cordova and famous artist
Sourdough – A nickname for someone that spends the entire winter north of the Arctic Circle (also a name used for long-time Alaskans)

COMPREHENSION QUESTIONS

1) How old was Eustace Paul Ziegler when he arrived in Cordova? Why did he travel there? ____

____

____

____

2) Describe the Red Dragon. What kind of people did it attract? ______________________

____

____

____

____

3) How did one painting for sale in a drug store change the direction of Eustace Paul Ziegler's life? ____

____

____

____

____

4) What kind of subjects did Eustace Paul Ziegler paint? Which famous mountain was one of his favorite subjects to paint? ______________________________

____

____

____

____

____

____

DISCUSSION QUESTION

(Discuss this question with your teacher or write your answer in essay form below. Use additional paper if necessary.)

One of Eustace Paul Ziegler's famous quotes was, "If you don't paint for money, you'll make money." What do you think he meant by this statement?

LEARN MORE

Read more about Eustace Paul Ziegler and other artists who found their inspiration in Alaska by visiting http://www.akhistorycourse.org/americas-territory/alaskas-heritage/chapter-4-19-art-literature-science-cultural-institutions-and-recreation

TIME TO REVIEW

Review Chapters 20-25 of your book before moving on the Unit Review. See how many questions you can answer without looking at your book.

This photo of Eustace Paul Ziegler, 87, was taken shortly before his death in 1969.

Early Alaska Trailblazers

Crossword Puzzle

Read Across and Down clues and fill in blank boxes that match numbers on the clues

Across

2 Mayo's name is associated with this village
4 Russian governor who forbade anyone from leaking information about gold being found in Alaska
6 Ancestry of Robert Service
9 Eustace Paul Ziegler drew artistic scenes upon these
10 Distributing point for people exploring possibilities of fur and gold along the Yukon River
14 This was the first building in Cordova
20 Ed Schieffelin's sternwheeler that became a supply carrier for trading posts
22 Eustace Paul Ziegler's profession when he arrived in Cordova in the early 1900s
23 People who wander from place to place without a home or job
25 Traders and prospectors hunted this wild animal for its meat
26 A poem or song narrating a story in short verse
28 People who mine for gold and other precious metals
29 A person living in unsettled country
32 Settlement where McQuestern said he and his companions were treated like kings
33 Editor of the *Whitehorse Star* who encouraged Robert Service
34 One of three men who became traders in the Yukon Basin in the 1870s
35 He was known as the voice of the Yukon
36 The meager stores along the Yukon River in the 1870s belonged to this company

Down

1 He was the first to discover gold in the Yukon in the 1870s
3 People who buy and sell goods
5 When Robert Service was transferred from Whitehorse to this town he found himself a celebrity in the eyes of the townspeople
7 A person who makes a new track through wild country
8 Fort that McQuestern established in 1870s six miles down from where Dawson was born in the 1890s
11 A person who is among the first to explore or settle a new country or area
12 People Robert Service found when he arrived in Whitehorse in early 1900s
13 A newcomer or novice, especially a person unaccustomed to the hardships of pioneer life
15 One of three men who became traders in the Yukon Basin in the 1870s
16 Another term for Alaska
17 Nickname of Episcopal mission in Cordova
18 Man who convinced Ziegler to follow his passion for painting

Early Alaska Trailblazers

Crossword Puzzle

Down (Continued)

19 Eustace Paul Ziegler became famous for doing this activity
21 Famous poem written by Robert Service
24 An old-timer in Alaska is called this
27 Writing that is arranged with a metrical rhythm, typically having a rhyme
30 A group of lines forming the basic recurring metrical unit in a poem
31 Eustace Paul Ziegler was known as this to everyone who knew him

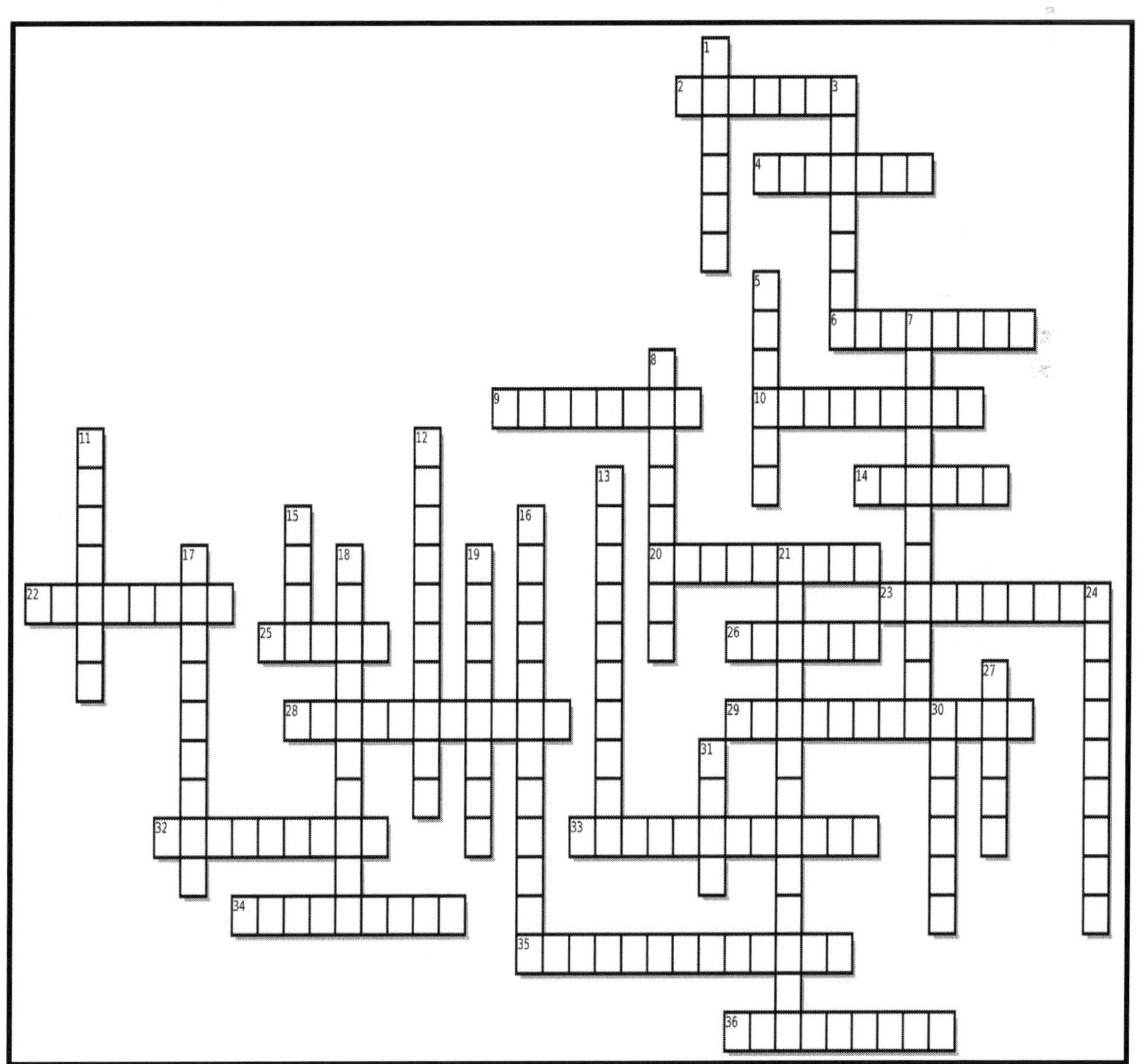

UNIT 6: WILDERNESS TRAILS
UNIT 7: A FEW TRAILBLAZERS

REVIEW LESSONS 20-25

Write down what you remember about:

Sled dog team ______________________________

____

Lead dog ______________________________

____

Iditarod Trail ______________________________

____

Walter Goodwin ______________________________

____

Tributary ______________________________

____

Arthur Harper ______________________________

____

Jack McQuesten ______________________________

____

Alfred Mayo ______________________________

____

Robert Service ______________________________

____

Whitehorse ______________________________

____

Eustace Paul Ziegler ______________________________

____

Sourdough ______________________________

____

Fill in the blanks:

1) ______________ of Alaska, northern ______________, Greenland and Siberia used dogs as ________________ for centuries. ______________ arriving in western Alaska during the 1700-1800s found ______________ using dogs to haul sleds loaded with fish, game, wood and other items.

2) Early ________________ fur traders added _____________ to sleds and trained ____________ dogs in order to use dog teams as a means of transportation through Alaska's wilderness.

3) When gold was discovered along the _________________ River around 1906-1907, another trail was forged that would become one of the most famous ________________ trails in history – the ____________ Trail.

4) Maj. Wilds P. Richardson ordered __________________ to blaze a route from _______________ through the Cook Inlet country and beyond to ___________. From January to April 1908, _____________ and a three-man crew scouted and blazed a trail from ____________ to Susitna and then west through Rainy Pass, across the Kuskokwim Valley to the ___________ Mining District, which included Ophir, McGrath and Takotna. They then angled the trail _______________ across the marshy lowlands of the Innoko Valley and connected with the _______________ trail at Kaltag.

5) The town of ____________ grew out of the wilderness after prospectors ___________ ____________ and _________________________ discovered gold along the Haiditarod River, a ______________ of the Innoko, in December 1908.

6) Three early pioneers, _______________________, _______________________ and ______________________ traveled into Alaska's interior and found a lack of _________________________________. Had they not seen the need to establish ______________________ in the wilderness, it is possible that ______________ to the Yukon and Alaska would not have boomed.

7) When they attempted to obtain information about the ____________________ of the Yukon River, they found little knowledge had been gleaned since __________________ occupation. By 1873, less than a dozen white men inhabited the length of the Yukon, and they were concerned with __________, not gold.

8) As ____________________ looked out the windows of the train heading to _____________________ from _________________, he viewed the rugged trail that led to the Klondike gold fields. The sensitive young man found it a thrilling environment and began to write ______________describing the ___________ Country. He was asked to write a ________ to recite at a ___________ function.

9) He wrote something every day on his lonely ___________ along the trails. He looked forward to those __________, he said, because he knew the ______________________________, and he would bubble verse like an artesian well, composing "The ______________ of the Yukon" and many other ballads.

10) ________________________________ was only 22 years of age when he arrived in __________________ to take charge of its Episcopal mission nicknamed the ___________________. He decorated the walls of the _______________, and the church that was later built, with _________________ of great beauty and deep religious feeling.

11) The president of the _______________________________asked Ziegler to ______________________________ for the company's Seattle office. When the _____________________ were completed, the Zieglers returned to _________________, but new offers flooded the little Alaskan minister. He finally had to make a choice between the _______________ and a career as an _________________.

12) One of his most famous ____________ was the "_________________." The ______________ mother and her placid _________ won innumerable prizes and hung in many galleries. His sympathy and affection for the _____________ people of Alaska shines through his ________________.

Traders like Jack McQuesten, pictured here in the early 1900s, made it possible for prospectors to get supplies and that allowed them to continue their search for gold.

UNIT 6: WILDERNESS TRAILS
UNIT 7: A FEW TRAILBLAZERS

UNIT TEST

Choose *three* of the following questions to answer in paragraph form. Use as much detail as possible to completely answer the question. Use extra paper in back of the book if needed.

1) Why were sled dog teams an important means of travel in early Alaska? Name some of the ways that they were utilized.

2) What important trail was Walter Goodwin hired to scout in Alaska? Why is this trail one of the most famous trails in Alaska history? Where did it start and end?

3) What need did Jack McQuesten, Al Mayo and Arthur Harper fill in the Yukon? Why was this vital to the success of the gold rush?

4) How did Robert Service begin his poetry career? How did he go about writing his poetry? Name two of his famous poems.

5) Describe Eustace Paul Ziegler's journey from missionary to Cordova to painter. What kind of paintings was he famous for?

UNIT 6: WILDERNESS TRAILS
UNIT 7: A FEW TRAILBLAZERS

Review Questions	______	(possible 12 pts.)
Fill-the-Blanks	______	(possible 12 pts.)

Unit Test

Essay 1

Demonstrates understanding of the topic	______	(possible 5 pts.)
Answered the questions completely and accurately	______	(possible 5 pts.)
Composition is neat	______	(possible 5 pts.)
Grammar and Spelling	______	(possible 5 pts.)

Essay 2

Demonstrates understanding of the topic	______	(possible 5 pts.)
Answered the questions completely and accurately	______	(possible 5 pts.)
Composition is neat	______	(possible 5 pts.)
Grammar and Spelling	______	(possible 5 pts.)

Essay 3

Demonstrates understanding of the topic	______	(possible 5 pts.)
Answered the questions completely and accurately	______	(possible 5 pts.)
Composition is neat	______	(possible 5 pts.)
Grammar and Spelling	______	(possible 5 pts.)

Subtotal Points ______ (possible 84 pts.)

Extra Credit

Word Puzzle	______	(5 pt. per completed puzzle)
Complete an Enrichment Activity	______	(possible 5 pts.)
Oral presentation	______	(possible 10 pts.)

Total Extra Credit ______

Total Unit Points ______

GRADE CHART

A 75-84+ points

B 67-75 points

C 58-66 points

D 49-57 points

UNIT 8: MIGHTY MOUNTAINS

LESSON 26: ELIAS – TOUGH EVERY FOOT OF THE WAY

FACTS TO KNOW

Mount St. Elias – The second-highest mountain in North America – it is located on the border of the Yukon and Alaska
Summit – The peak of a mountain
Israel Cook Russell – The first to explore Alaska for the U.S. Geological Survey
The Duke of Abruzzi – The first to summit Mount St. Elias

COMPREHENSION QUESTIONS

1) Who was the first non-Native to spot Mount St. Elias? When did he first see it and name it for Russia? ______________________________

____

____

2) What important areas are located around Mount St. Elias? ______________

____

____

3) How tall is Mount St. Elias? Why is it considered one of the greatest snow climbs in the world? ______________________________

____

____

4) Although Israel Cook Russell never reached the peak of Mount St. Elias, what important discoveries and accomplishments did he make on his two trips?

____

____

____

5) Who was the first to summit Mount St. Elias? When? How long was the expedition?

____

____

____

6) Why did Asa C. Baldwin lead a party to climb Mount St. Elias? What was different about his approach to the mountain? ________________________________

____

____

____

DISCUSSION QUESTION

(Discuss this question with your teacher or write your answer in essay form below. Use additional paper if necessary.)

Climbing large mountains like Mount St. Elias is a dangerous endeavor. What were some of the challenges that the climbers faced?

____

____

____

____

____

____

____

____

____

____

____

____

____

____

ENRICHMENT ACTIVITY

Imagine that you are a mountaineer who is preparing to summit a mountain. Considering what you have learned from this lesson, what do you need to do to prepare? What type of supplies do you need to bring with you? Write a short paragraph about how you will prepare for your upcoming climb.

LEARN MORE

Look for this article at your local library:
"Wrangell-Saint Elias: International Mountain Wilderness," Alaska Geographic Society, Vol. 8, No. 1, 1981.

UNIT 8: MIGHTY MOUNTAINS

LESSON 27: DENALI – THE HIGH ONE

FACTS TO KNOW

Denali – Also known as "Mount McKinley," this is the highest mountain in North America

Dr. Frederick A. Cook – Controversial mountaineer who claimed to have summited Denali and discovered the North Pole

Admiral Robert E. Peary – U.S. Navy engineer who claimed to be the discoverer of the North Pole

Walter Harper – An Athabascan Indian, he was the first person known to have climbed to the summit of Denali

COMPREHENSION QUESTIONS

1) Who named Mount McKinley? Why did he choose this name? Why is the name controversial? ____

____

____

____

2) Who was the first white man to climb Mount McKinely? How did he and his companions raise money for the trip? ______________________________

____

____

____

3) In 1903, ______________________ and five team members reached the 11,300-foot level of __________________. He and a team returned in 1906 to climb it again. Cook later reported that he had summited __________________ that time. After returning from Alaska,______________ gave lectures about his achievement – including one in Seattle that started the organization of ________________________. He left his 1903 and 1906 book manuscripts with a publisher in 1907 and then headed for Greenland, a trip that later evolved into an expedition to reach the _____________.

4) Why did some people doubt Dr. Frederick A. Cook's account of his expedition?

____

____

____

5) What led the Sourdough Party to decide to climb Denali? ____________________

____

____

6) Who was the first person to summit Denali? Who led his team, and why did this man refuse to call the mountain Mount McKinley? ______________________________

____

____

DISCUSSION QUESTION

(Discuss this question with your teacher or write your answer in essay form below. Use additional paper if necessary.)

In 2015, the U.S. Geological Survey announced that new measurements put Denali's height at 20,310 feet, 10 feet shorter than previously measured. That same year, President Barack Obama officially changed the name of the mountain to Denali. Do you think it matters whether we call the mountain Denali or Mount McKinley? Explain your answer.

____

____

____

____

____

____

____

____

ENRICHMENT ACTIVITY

Learn more about Denali National Park by watching this 5-minute video on YouTube: https://www.youtube.com/watch?v=TiJtxItuC18

LEARN MORE

Look for this book at your local library:
The Ascent of Denali, Hudson Stuck. Seattle: The Mountaineer, 1977.

UNIT 8: MIGHTY MOUNTAINS

LESSON 28: KATMAI ERUPTS

FACTS TO KNOW

Novarupta – Volcano in Southwest Alaska that erupted in 1912 and was largest volcanic eruption of the 20th Century

Mount Katmai – One of five vents encircling the Novarupta volcano that has a central lake-filled caldera formed during the Novarupta explosion

Dora – Little mail boat that brought the first news of the eruption to the outside world

Kodiak – The closest sizeable town that was only 120 miles away from the eruption

Valley of 10,000 Smokes – The valley within Katmai National Park and Preserve that is filled with ash flow from the eruption of Novarupta June 6–8, 1912

COMPREHENSION QUESTIONS

1) Who were the only eyewitnesses to the volcanic eruption in 1912? How many people lost their lives during the eruption? ____

____

____

____

2) Describe what some of the eyewitnesses saw and heard during the Novarupta blast.

____

____

____

____

3) Where was the *Dora* sailing when its crew spotted the eruption? Describe the crew's account. ____

____

____

____

4) What horrible experience did the people of Kodiak endure when Novarupta erupted?
____
____
____

5) U.S. Revenue Cutter ________________ carried more than 500 residents of ___________ and _________________ to safe waters during ________________ _________________. The priest of the Greek Orthodox Church told his people that if the ____________________________________ they were to go down to the dock.

6) Who was the man that made the Valley of 10,000 Smokes known to the world? What are two things that we learned from him? __________________________________
____
____

DISCUSSION QUESTION

(Discuss this question with your teacher or write your answer in essay form below. Use additional paper if necessary.)

Imagine that you lived in Kodiak at the time of the eruption at Katmai. Remembering the accounts that you read in your lesson, how do you think you would have felt during and after the eruption? Can you imagine experiencing constant darkness like they did?

____
____
____
____
____
____
____
____
____

LEARN MORE

Explore the Valley of 10,000 Smokes by visiting https://www.nps.gov/katm/planyour-visit/exploring-the-valley-of-ten-thousand-smokes.htm

TIME TO REVIEW

Review Chapters 26-28 of your book before moving on the Unit Review. See how many questions you can answer without looking at your book.

UNIT 8: MIGHTY MOUNTAINS

REVIEW LESSONS 26-29

Write down what you remember about:

Mount St. Elias ______________________________

____

Summit ______________________________

____

Israel Cook Russell ______________________________

____

The Duke of Abruzzi ______________________________

____

Denali ______________________________

____

Dr. Frederick A. Cook ______________________________

____

Admiral Robert E. Peary ______________________________

____

Walter Harper ______________________________

____

Novarupta ______________________________

____

Mount Katmai ______________________________

____

Dora ______________________________

____

Kodiak ______________________________

____

Valley of 10,000 Smokes ______________________________

____

Fill in the blanks:

1) __________________, the first point sighted by white men on the mainland of Alaska in 1741, has proved a mighty challenge to_______________________. Only a handful of climbers have conquered it in the years since the Dane, _________________________, discovered and named it for _________________________.

2) In 1890, professor __________________________ led a party composed of Mark B. Karr and six camp hands. Russell and Karr undoubtedly would have reached the top if a _______________________________ had not forced their retreat.

3) But the route that professor ________________________ had explored was of great assistance when, in 1897, the mountain finally was conquered by one of the world's most distinguished mountain climbers and explorers, ______________________________.

4) Rising more than 20,000 feet above sea level, a mountain known to early __________ Indians of the Interior as _______________, meaning "_______________," towers over all other peaks in its mountain range.

5) ______________________, a prospector, named the 20,310-foot mountain – which is said to have one of the earth's steepest vertical rises – for presidential nominee ______________________ of Ohio in 1896, even though he had no ties to __________.

6) At a dinner sponsored by the National Geographic Society, with a seething ___________________________ in attendance, President Theodore Roosevelt hailed __________________ as the conqueror of McKinley and the first American to explore both __________________. But critics soon denounced _________________ claim and suggested his summit photo of Ed Barrill was suspect.

7) The ______________________ were the only eyewitnesses to the most spectacular ______________________ to occur in North America during the 20th century. Native residents of ______________ village found their barabaras – Native dwellings – buried in ___________ from the 1912 ________________ of __________________.

8) The ___________, the intrepid little mail boat that had had a share in almost every adventure in _______________Alaska, brought the first news of the ________________ to the outside world. Crew members noticed a huge, dense ___________________rise over Mount ___________________. It spread northwestward over the sky and masses of ____________________ settled over the sea. It became so dense the captain had to bypass Kodiak.

9) A news dispatch from Cordova, 360 miles northeast of the _______________, reported that many people received ______________ when a heavy rain mixed with the _______ in the air to form sulfuric acid.

10) The closest sizable town, _____________, was 120 miles away from Mount ____________. Terror and fear held the island's 400 inhabitants. None of the people who went through those days fail to mention the awful ____________, which was described as something so far beyond the ________________________________ that it cannot be comprehended by those who did not experience it.

Courtesy University of Alaska Anchorage

The members of the 1919 National Geographic Expedition that explored the Katmai region following the eruption of 1912 found volcanic rocks, called pumice, so light that they could balance them on their legs.

Mighty Alaska Mountains

Word Scramble

Unscramble the words below

1. ituvs nigbre		This Danish explorer discovered and named Mount St. Elias for Russia in 1741
2. stcaahbana		Prehistoric and historic archeological sites of these Indians were discovered around Mount St. Elias
3. gsarciel		Rivers of ice
4. onintreemau		One who climbs mountains
5. wne royk simte		This company funded the first attempt to climb Mount St. Elias in 1886
6. ocrfcanes		This duke was the first man to summit Mount St. Elias in 1897
7. naffamuk		First woman to summit Mount St. Elias in 1946
8. eht ghhi one		The meaning of the Athabascan Indian word Denali
9. aalaks		Denali is part of this mountain range
10. rocaevvun		This English explorer made the first known reference to Denali in 1794

Mighty Alaska Mountains

Word Scramble - Continued

Unscramble the words below

11. dykeic	Prospector who gave the name Mount McKinley to what we call Denali in 1896
12. whkmiearcs	First white man to attempt to climb Denali in 1903
13. ocko	Controversy surrounds this mountaineer's claim that he reached the summit of Denali in 1906
14. gudsrhuoo patry	This group of men attempted to climb Denali in 1910 based on a wager
15. uodsnh ukstc	Episcopal archdeacon whose party was the first to reach the summit of Denali in 1913
16. rarphe	Name of Athabascan Indian who had the honor of being the first to step foot on the summit of Denali first
17. smtayaclc	A large-scale and violent event in the natural world
18. onarvpaut	Name of volcano that exploded in southwest Alaska in June 1912
19. odkaki	Name of town that was covered in ash for days following the eruption in Katmai
20. nngmnia	Name of ship that saved the people of Kodiak and Woody Island from the deadly ash that fell in June 1912 following the eruption of a volcano

UNIT 8: MIGHTY MOUNTAINS

UNIT TEST

Choose *two* of the following questions to answer in paragraph form. Use as much detail as possible to completely answer the question. Use extra paper in back of the book if needed.

1) Why was Mount St. Elias such a challenge for even experienced mountain climbers to summit? What were some of the challenges that the mountaineers had to face? Describe one expedition that you read about in Lesson 26. Was it successful?

2) Explain why the name "Mount McKinley" is controversial. What other controversy did you read about in Lesson 27?

3) What happened in Kodiak in the summer of 1912? Describe some of the eyewitness accounts you read in Lesson 28.

UNIT 8: MIGHTY MOUNTAINS

Review Questions	______	(possible 13 pts.)
Fill-the-Blanks	______	(possible 10 pts.)

Unit Test

Essay 1

Demonstrates understanding of the topic	______	(possible 5 pts.)
Answered the questions completely and accurately	______	(possible 5 pts.)
Composition is neat	______	(possible 5 pts.)
Grammar and Spelling	______	(possible 5 pts.)

Essay 2

Demonstrates understanding of the topic	______	(possible 5 pts.)
Answered the questions completely and accurately	______	(possible 5 pts.)
Composition is neat	______	(possible 5 pts.)
Grammar and Spelling	______	(possible 5 pts.)

Subtotal Points ______ (possible 63 pts.)

Extra Credit

Word Puzzle	______	(5 pt. per completed puzzle)
Complete an Enrichment Activity	______	(possible 5 pts.)
Oral presentation	______	(possible 10 pts.)

Total Extra Credit ______

Total Unit Points ______

GRADE CHART

A 57-63+ points

B 50-56 points

C 43-49 points

D 36-42 points

EXTRA PAPER FOR LESSONS

EXTRA PAPER FOR LESSONS

EXTRA PAPER FOR LESSONS

EXTRA PAPER FOR LESSONS

EXTRA PAPER FOR LESSONS

EXTRA PAPER FOR LESSONS

EXTRA PAPER FOR LESSONS